THE
COMEDY
MARKET

THE
COMEDY
MARKET

A Writer's Guide
to Making Money
Being Funny

Carmine DeSena

A PERIGEE BOOK

A Perigee Book
Published by The Berkley Publishing Group
200 Madison Avenue
New York, NY 10016

Copyright © 1996 by Carmine DeSena

Book design by Rhea Braunstein

Cover design by Dale Fiorillo

First edition: August 1996

Published simultaneously in Canada.

The Putnam Berkley World Wide Web site address is
http://www.berkley.com

Library of Congress Cataloging-in-Publication Data

DeSena, Carmine.
    The comedy market : a writer's guide to making money being
        funny /
Carmine DeSena. — 1st ed.
        p.   cm.
    "A Perigee book."
    Includes bibliographical references.
    ISBN 0-399-52215-8
    1. Comedy—Authorship. 2. Wit and humor—Authorship.
    3. Fiction—Authorship—Marketing. I. Title.
    PN6149.A88D47   1996
    808.7—dc20   95-52133
                                                                      CIP

Printed in the United States of America

10   9   8   7   6   5   4   3   2   1

Contents

Acknowledgments

I would like to thank the following individuals who provided me with resources, support, and insight into the business of humor writing: Arlen Appelbaum, Tiffany Dupree, Ina Greenfield, Thelma Leibowitz, Nat May, Willis Moore, Yvonne Negron, Genny Wilkinson, and Romona Wyche.

"Brevity is the soul of wit."
WILLIAM SHAKESPEARE, *Hamlet*

Introduction

"Real People Don't Become Writers"

This statement has haunted me my entire life. It kills the hopes and dreams that a creative person might have. Thank God I ignored it. Too bad I said it to begin with. After publishing four books, articles in *US* magazine, *The New York Times*, and *Theater Week*, and having my comedy writing heard nationwide on the ABC radio network, in comedy clubs, colleges, and cabarets, I realize real people do become writers. Who else is there?

Throughout college I vacillated between writing and a "real" 9-to-5 job, and finally opted for the easy road of 9 to 5 because of the aforementioned quote. I was wrong, and I couldn't be happier. The writing life has a certain mystique that makes it appear both attractive and unattainable. Exploring that mystique in an organized way is very telling. You discover it is attainable. That's what this book is about.

I want you to begin in the world of humor writing with the confidence and knowledge it took me over a decade to develop. In fact, I want you to have more. I have interviewed dozens of producers, editors, publishers, agents, executives and anyone else in the business of presenting humor material. I have mapped it out so simply, you can forget the compass; all you need is a word processor and your special comic voice.

Don't get me wrong; I can't teach you talent. In fact, this book is like your mother. It believes you have talent. And just like your mother, you won't believe everything the book tells you. But as you work in the business, you will realize the book was always right. And when you turn 60, you'll realize your mother was right too.

HOW TO USE THIS BOOK

This is a guide that explores each market for humor writing in chapters organized as follows:

- An explanation of each specific market.
- The opportunities that exist.
- Where to learn the techniques you need to turn your own voice into salable writing.
- Education and training.
- Networking and breaking into the business.
- Representation.
- Submitting the material.

Included are in-depth looks at stand-up comedy, cable and network television, screenwriting, playwriting, humor books and novel writing, magazine and newspaper work, radio comedy, the greeting card business, and humor writing for corporate clients.

While I believe all of this will be tremendously helpful, I still don't think it's enough. This book also covers a few topics you probably haven't thought about—grants and contests and education alternatives, for instance. The time to learn about these things is *before* you need them, and the resources listed in the appendices of this book will tell you how to access them in an affordable way from anywhere in the country. That's right! You don't have to live in New York or L.A. Sure, after you're making money you may have to be where the action is. But isn't it better to relocate after you begin to establish yourself?

Let me start by revealing what every successful humor writer I spoke with has integrated into their professional life. More than helpful tips, these are writers' affirmations. You should repeat them to yourself constantly and incorporate them into your writing life.

- Don't wait for a door to open. Use virtually every window, side door, and crawl space to get into the business.
- Put yourself out there in a big way! Hang out at comedy clubs, festivals, hip eateries or any place where the people who are doing what you want to do hang out.
- Discover and use the theory of "six degrees of separation." Develop and maintain networks of friends and acquaintances who might know someone who can help get you to where you want to be.
- Remember the names of important people and get to know their assistants as well. The first cable

TV writing job I got came from a recommendation from an assistant to an agent I wasn't even signed with. He calls me his first client. I call him . . . regularly.

- Immerse yourself in the writing markets and the industry trades, as well as the world around you. Read newspapers and magazines, watch the shows . . . know everything.
- Interpret rejection as a challenge.
- Realize that no one will look after your interests better than yourself. Even though you may use an agent, manager, and/or lawyer, know your way around a contract or a negotiation.
- Try various forms of writing until you find a niche, or a series of niches that make the best use of your talent.

AND MOST IMPORTANT!

- *Write and write and write*. Even without a sale or recognition of any kind, perfect your craft. Not because you like to write, but because you are compulsive about it.

A PRACTICAL APPROACH

If knowledge is power, having all the information gives you control. That's why a practical approach is so important. If you integrate these writing affirmations and use the strategies outlined in this book, *you* will be in control of your career.

Given the information here, you will learn not to sit around and wait for something to happen—you will make it happen! You have to take responsibility for your career as you would for any commitment about which you feel strongly. You make things happen by having the information you need, polishing your skills, and making contacts. So read on. In fact, read through the whole book initially to get an overview of the business as a whole. It will give you insight into the various forms of humor writing and help you select an area to begin working on.

Chapter 1

The Stand-up Connection:

Performing and Networking Your Way Into a Writing Job

NOW APPEARING

JEFF ROSS
TV credits: Comedy Central, *MTV Half Hour Comedy Hour*, *Caroline's Comedy Hour* (the Arts and Entertainment network), and *Evening at the Improv*

JOHN TEN EYCK
TV credits: *MTV Half Hour Comedy Hour*, *Remote Control*, and *Bugged!* (America's Talking Network)
Improvisation: Chicago City Limits

DAVE ATTELL
TV credits: David Letterman, Conan O'Brien, *Stand-Up Spotlight*, *Caroline's Comedy Hour*

JEFF CLINKENBEARD
TV credits: Producer's Assistant, *House of Buggin'*; Writers' Assistant, *Cheers* and *Frasier*
Improvisation: New York Improv Squad and Chicago City Limits

RICK DORFMAN
Personal Manager, Jay Mohr (*Saturday Night Live*), Red Johnny and the Round Guy (MTV), Wally Collins (Host of *Stand-Up Stand-Up*), Mario Cantone (Steam Pipe Alley), Jim Breuer (Up Town Comedy Club)

• • •

One sure way of getting your humor writing before an audience is to do it yourself, the stand-up comedy way. While many writers may experience more stage fright than success, there are a variety of benefits to performing stand-up comedy, even if you don't want a career in front of an audience. These include:

- Learning comic timing and developing your own voice.
- Increasing your knowledge of the business.
- Creating opportunities to write for other performers.
- Collaborating with other professionals.
- Becoming more adept at pitching ideas to television and film executives.
- Networking with producers, agents, comics, and other people in the business who scour the clubs in search of talent.
- Gaining exposure to press and industry people.

THERE'S NOTHING LIKE AN AUDIENCE TO TELL YOU WHAT'S FUNNY!
STAND-UP COMEDY . . . AND WHY IT'S IMPORTANT FOR EVERY HUMOR WRITER

The highlight of my stand-up career was appearing at the Comic Strip in New York City. This was a big step for me after doing an open-mike show at a bagel store. (I'll have a career with a schmeer.) Both of these experiences were amazingly helpful to my writing. Even if you decide never to perform, becoming a regular on the scene can have a huge impact on your work. Seeing hundreds of comics perform will give you a sense of what a comic voice is. You will see different interpretations of the same material and develop a feeling for comic timing. Analyze why some comics are funnier than others and how their material is affected by presentation. This is basically the character of the performer. Ask yourself whether the material stands up on its own. These are questions that you will face in your own development as a writer.

From my own experience I learned that nothing tells you if something is funny better than an audience. I am often amazed at what an audience responds to or rejects. After years of writing, this hasn't changed. An audience gives you immediate feedback, which is crucial in developing your own voice. If you stray too far, the audience will not follow. When you write for other markets, most of the time you will be working in a vacuum. Performing stand-up comedy gives you a valuable chance to explore what is funny and special about your voice and create a repertoire of audience-tested material.

THE MARKET

From vaudeville to the Catskills, and from Ed Sullivan to David Letterman, the stand-up comic has always held a high-priority spot in entertainment. Cable stand-up shows and network sitcoms still dominate television. Remember, all of these performers started at the same level—the open-mike night of a comedy club. Comic performers will usually climb the ranks through a series of steps that more or less take this form:

1. Open mike.
2. Showcase clubs/benefits.
3. Paid clubs/parties.
4. Colleges.
5. Radio.
6. TV.
7. Film—you should be so lucky!

Each of these steps is absolutely critical. As the comedian moves to the next level, the stakes increase. As you progress, you need more material. Then you need better material and a more polished performance style, and so forth. That's why it pays to start at the bottom and work your way up even if you plan to be a writer and not perform yourself. Don't forget the most important writer's affirmation: Write and write and write to perfect your craft. If you perform mediocre material or offer it to an established professional, you risk losing a vital networking opportunity. Take the time to do the work, and when an opportunity arises, you will be ready for it.

As you contemplate writing for your stand-up act, remember that the material is meant to be heard, not read. Practice doing your act out loud. Expect your first performance to bomb! You have two strikes against you: You have not done stand-up before, and your material is untested. Expect to bomb again and again. When you find the experience so horrible that you can't possibly do it again—force yourself to go on one more time. Get on stage any way possible. Every comedian I've known has started off terribly. Some get better, some don't develop much, and some stay terrible. In the end, people may say that the only reason you should ever be on stage is to sweep. Don't let comments like that deter you. Be tenacious. Alter your material to get a better response and practice your delivery. You may have to write ten or twenty bits or more before you get a good joke. As with any writing, the emphasis should be on the rewrites.

INSIDE VIEW

- Get on stage as much as possible to improve performing, timing, and material.
- Write every day—constantly.
- Have a sense of truth about yourself and your material.
- Record every performance you do to listen, learn, and improve.

—RICK DORFMAN

The best route to learning about stand-up comedy involves going to open-mike clubs and scoping out the atmosphere. Watch what the other comics are doing and figure out who makes up the audience. Evaluate the general feeling of the room. Open-mike nights abound in every city in the country. After my stint at the bagel store, I was asked to perform in the back of a hardware store. This was quite a step up for me. I was now working retail. Obviously, open-mike clubs are not the best environments, but they are great places to learn and try new material. If you go to an established club and bomb, you may never have a chance to get booked there again.

Work toward building a solid ten minutes, then add new material in between your stronger jokes. You should continue this process of constantly developing material. As you progress up the food chain of comedy clubs, you will need to have longer sets of material than the brief couple of minutes that made you a star in the open-mike rooms.

Showcase clubs such as the Improv in Los Angeles or the Comic Strip in New York City are venues where industry people scout for comics for television or writing jobs. Audition spots at showcase clubs are hard to come by. You will probably have to audition several times before getting a regular performance time. At this point, you should have developed a strong hour of material, and performance and timing should be more consistent. If these elements are all in sync, agents and talent bookers will take notice and make it possible for you to move on to paying gigs at road clubs, private functions, or colleges.

At this level, constantly developing new material should be your biggest concern. By the time radio and television bookings begin, you'll realize just how quickly the media eats material.

LEARNING TO WRITE FOR OTHER PEOPLE

If you have chosen to focus on writing instead of performing, begin by watching other comics on stage and put these observations to work. Try writing material for them based on what you've seen. Keep in mind their delivery styles and points of view. Try to capture the focus of their stage persona. If you aspire to write for television, film, or theater, this exercise will help you write for characters and maintain the consistency of their voices. You may decide to begin to offer your work to the comics you have been observing. If they are beginners, they may not be able to pay you (it never hurts to ask). This will allow you to network with your colleagues in the business while developing your writing skills. When these comics start to get work that involves long sets or television spots that really eat material, you will be in a position to make money and earn writing credits.

If you are writing for a reasonably established comic, never sign away material for free. Someone you write for may move up the career ladder and want to use the material on television or for a high-paying college gig. If they are being compensated, so should you be.

EDUCATION AND TRAINING

None of the people I interviewed recommended a stand-up comedy class as a starting point for beginners. I never enrolled in such a class. I do think, however, it can be worthwhile if you feel you need a structured program that would help guide you through the steps of preparing and polishing a performance. Classes are usually offered at comedy clubs and acting schools. Find a class that prepares you to do a set and satisfies the following criteria:

- It should teach you to write from the heart. Personalizing your delivery and material will make you stand out.
- The teacher should have a strong performance background and offer insight into stage performance. If possible, see him (or his students) perform before enrolling.
- The class should explore the rhythm and timing of stand-up performing.
- It should culminate in a performance at a professional space—the true test is *always* an audience.

INSIDE VIEW

"Just do it! If you want to do stand-up, you just have to do it. The same is true of writing."

—DAVE ATTEL

ACTING CLASSES

In acting class, they say you have to "know yourself." It's a cliché, but it's true. This applies to both writing and performing stand-up. Since acting training is an introspective process, you learn to use yourself and your emotions to bring a sense of realism to your work. Understanding the basics of acting will also give you insight on how to write for performers. When you know what an actor can bring to a role, you can write with more balance and confidence.

THE PERFORMANCE ALTERNATIVE: IMPROVISATION

Stand-up experience is invaluable, but studying and performing with an improvisation ensemble can really fine-tune your writing skills. Having done this myself for five years on the club scene and college circuit, I can vouch that it has kept me from ever suffering writer's block. It has given me the power to let my mind think expansively without overintellectualizing. My material is more organic.

The ensemble nature of improvisation is more scriptlike, and you need to have excellent scene-building skills to perform improvisation successfully. As a former improvisation performer and teacher, I was lucky enough to have the rules of improvisation reinforced for me constantly. These rules include:

- *Don't deny.* In improvisation, if you deny the information offered, then the scene stops. For example:

  1st Person: *Dad, I've decided I'm going to run away from home.*

  2nd Person: *I'm not your father. I'm a plumber.*

  If this were to happen, how could this scene continue? It would be a series of false starts. If the second person agrees, the scene can move ahead.

  1st Person: *Dad, I've decided I'm going to run away from home.*

  2nd Person: *Great, I'll come with you!*

INSIDE VIEW

"Improvisation is much better than stand-up for writing because it teaches you to write structurally as opposed to 'joke-wise.' You learn that humor can come out of a situation as opposed to a moment. You can't just go for a joke because you have to do a scene. You therefore learn to develop a scene. Everyone should take these classes. They don't have to be good at it, but it's a thought process that will help their writing."

—JOHN TEN EYCK

- *Listen.* To advance a scene and keep it consistent you must pay attention to dialogue. Good dialogue follows logically and organically. Each new line should follow the logic of the previous line.
- *Use the first suggestion.* Good improvisational performers make it a die-hard rule to use the first suggestion that they hear from the audience as a starting point. This teaches you to think creatively about each idea.

Improvisation companies offer classes, but you can also find them at acting schools and comedy clubs. Since the nature of improvisation is to create on the spot, the scenes and dialogue are always new. Many comics and writers continue to study to keep themselves fresh. As a former student and instructor, I suggest that the best way to assess whether a class is useful is to see if the teaching emphasizes the rules I've highlighted.

INSIDE VIEW

"There's a lot of bad improvisation out there. Before you choose a place to study, see the company show. If the show is bad, how good can the classes be?"

—JEFF CLINKENBEARD

BREAKING INTO WRITING

Television is a big market for comedy writers. Most people don't realize that all shows—talk shows, sitcoms, game shows, even award shows—need writers. Even if you can't land a staff job, there's always the possibility of finding freelance work. In order to be asked to submit and pitch material, you need to network aggressively. Performing stand-up, especially in cities such as New York and L.A., puts you out there in a big way. At this point, all the years of performing in seedy clubs for three people at two A.M. pays off, providing that you've worked on your writing steadily. But if you haven't put in the time, this exposure will work against you.

INSIDE VIEW

"You have to keep developing your work so you're ready when the time comes. In my experience, you only have one chance to impress people. People form an opinion of you and that's it. I've seen it happen when I've worked on shows. They'll be looking for writers and someone's name would come up. Then someone else on the show would say, 'I've seen him or read his work and he sucks.' And for that performer, it's over."

—JOHN TEN EYCK

PITCHING

Taking the time to polish your writing and performing skills will ensure that when your name comes up within industry circles the consensus will be positive. This expertise will also foster your ability to present your ideas verbally. This is crucial for television assignments, during which writers work on scripts in groups, shouting out ideas at a feverish pace. Honing your verbal skills will also prepare you for your initial meetings with producers, where you'll be expected to pitch script ideas in a short, concise format.

Pitching involves a meeting between a writer and a producer during which ideas for television shows or other projects are presented verbally. Your ability to relate these ideas is as crucial as the ideas themselves. If you don't present them well, you can't expect that anyone will understand them or believe you can produce quality work. Appearing night after night before an audience gives stand-up comics an edge in presenting their ideas verbally at a pitch session.

INSIDE VIEW

"If you can be comfortable with an audience, you can be comfortable with a group of people at a pitch meeting. Stand-up gives you more confidence when you pitch because pitching is a performance."

—JOHN TEN EYCK

13

Inside View

"The first show I got called in for was an MTV sketch show. I was nervous, but it's a natural progression when you're doing stand-up to go into sketch comedy. I was in Boston working at a club when I got a call from the MTV talent coordinator saying that a couple of people had mentioned my name. She asked me to come in on Monday and pitch. Now it's Friday and I'm working all weekend, so I write all day and try the ideas on my friends. I know the stuff is funny. I drive home and put the stuff on the computer. The next day I'm at MTV. I get to the session and I'm sitting in a big conference room with nine people and I didn't know who anyone was or the chain of command. I know I'm doing well, getting laughs, but there was one guy who I was sure was the head writer, and he wasn't laughing. He looked bored, restless, and like he wanted to get out of there, but I keep going. I feel I'm still doing well and was about to pitch my last idea when someone comes in and tells this guy he's got a phone call. Now I'm really pissed off because he's taking a call. He mumbles into the phone, then stands up and says, 'I have to leave, the contractions are three minutes apart.' I broke up laughing. No wonder he wasn't listening."

—JEFF ROSS

The most important aspect of pitching is confidence. You'll need to be confident—especially if you find yourself in a room surrounded by a group of intimidating industry people who don't look like they want to be there.

Pitching is an essential skill for writers who work on sitcoms, sketch comedy shows, and other television comedy vehicles. Given the dozen or so writers on sketch shows, demonstrating a strength for pitching guarantees a writer's visibility. Even the best ideas can't be developed if they are not communicated well.

INSIDE VIEW

"When I worked on *Saturday Night Live*, we had to pitch sketches constantly to the head writer and guest host. For me that was the most fun—it was like performing. I could come up with things off the top of my head, like doing stand-up."

—DAVE ATTELL

AGENTS AND MANAGERS

Wearing the two hats of writer and performer makes selecting an agent or manager difficult. When you take full responsibility for your career, you may have questions or expectations based on what you know about the business. Often, when an agent and manager takes you on, they don't like to be told what to do or even receive phone calls from you. In their defense, however, there are tons of writers and performers who know *nothing*, but have ideas and dreams about *everything*. I worked with one agent who found my suggestions helpful. But my suggestions were based on research, not opinions I put together. In short, you need to gauge just what is the *right* amount of communication. Obviously, if you are making money for the agent you will have more clout with him than if you are an unproven entity. Being responsible for your career involves you not being led like a little lamb (and you know where they wind up), and it also asks that you do your homework and make tough choices.

Never assume that an agent who can book you as a stand-up comic can also secure television writing jobs for you. All agents are limited to the relationships, contacts, and influence they have in each individual market. It is important to select people to represent you in the areas in which they have the strongest connections.

INSIDE VIEW

"When I was getting an agent I told him I didn't know how good he was because we were in New York and all the big deals were in L.A. and he said, 'And L.A. stands for . . . ?' I have different agents who specialize in college dates, literary work, acting, stand-up, and writing."

—JEFF ROSS

Like agents, personal managers find work for their clients, but they also help to develop, create, and nurture their clients' careers. Managers use their contacts to help package a client's act or pitch a client's ideas to television producers. In addition, they offer business and financial advice.

Stand-up comics have an edge when it comes to meeting agents and personal managers. Writing is a solitary job that keeps you tied to your computer. Doing stand-up puts you out there where you can be seen. It will take time to get noticed, but when you're ready, agents and managers will seek you out. They won't waste their time with newcomers who haven't proven their talent or determination.

As a writer/performer you should not only take the time to develop your talent, but you should get to know which agents and managers are reputable. When you meet with agents or managers, maintain your composure and professionalism. If you get too desperate around an agent or any industry person, you'll get the cold shoulder.

Even if you are cautious, you still could find yourself in the hands of an irresponsible agent or manager. Many big-name celebrities have suffered from bad representation. Know what you're signing, and don't give anyone carte blanche with your time, money or any aspect of your career as a writer or performer. You may get ripped off, but you *need* representation for people to take you seriously. You also need a buffer between you and your employers, whose contracts can be even more exploitative. Never forget that this is a business, and everyone is trying to make the biggest profit margin. Always have any agreement or contract reviewed by your own attorney. Utilize Appendix IV: Legal Issues on page 201 to learn about how to protect your work—and your career.

RESOURCES

Directories

The Comedy USA Guide, Murray Hill Station, P.O. Box 990, New York NY l0156. Tel: 212-532-0171. Published yearly, this trade directory contains information on contacting talent agencies, management, comedy clubs, and booking agents and other professionals in the stand-up comedy business. An invaluable resource, especially if you are living outside a major city and need to learn about networking possibilities.

The Drama Book Shop, Inc., 723 7th Avenue, New York NY 10019. Tel: 212-944-0595 or toll-free at 800-322-0595. This company offers an extensive mail order catalog of books dealing with all areas of networking, performing, and writing.

Organizations

Professional Comedian's Association, 581 9th Avenue, Suite #3C, New York NY 10036. Tel: 212-623-5233 or 800-YES-YUKS. This organization provides members with legal counsel, health and dental benefits, an informative newsletter, discounts on phone use and car rental, and other necessities for the traveling stand-up. It also offers tax guides for the freelancer, a pension plan, and a contact list.

Books

The Last Laugh: The World of Stand-Up Comics by Phil Berger. $14.95. Limelight Editions, 118 E. 30th St., New York NY 10016. An insider's look at the world of stand-up comedy performers and clubs.

The Stand-Up Comedy Book by Judy Carter. $12.95. A Dell trade paperback. Bantam Doubleday Dell Publishing Group, Inc., 1540 Broadway, New York NY 10036. An insightful book that takes you into the inner workings of the stand-up comedy world.

Improv: Improvisation and the Theater by Keith Johnstone. $14.95. Routledge, Chapman & Hall, Inc., 29 W. 35th St., New York NY 10001. One of the true masters of improvisation reviews skills and applications.

Comic Lives: The World of American Stand-Up Comedy by Betsy Borns. $8.95. A Fireside book. Simon & Schuster, 1230 Avenue of the Americas, New York NY 10020. Informative interviews with the most successful stand-up comedians in the industry.

Comedy Writing by Gene Peret. $11.95. Samuel French, Inc., 7623 Sunset Blvd., Hollywood CA 90046. Sensible advice on how to write and sell humor by one of the pillars of the comedy writing community.

Chapter 2

The TV Guide:

Writing for the Network and Cable Television Markets

FEATURING

GLORIA BANTA
Vice President of Development, Comedy Central
Staff Writer, *The Mary Tyler Moore Show, Cagney & Lacey*

JEFF ROSS
Writer, *Which Way to the Super Bowl* (NBC) and *Red Johnny and the Round Guy* (MTV)

DAVE ATTELL
Writer, *Caroline's Comedy Hour* (A&E), *Saturday Night Live* (NBC), *The Jon Stewart Show*

JOHN TEN EYCK
Writer, *Remote Control, Spring Break, The MTV Beach House, Like We Care, Lip Service, Amuck in America* (all MTV), *Rumor Has It* (VH-1), *Double Dare* (Nickelodeon), *Where in the World Is Carmen Sandiego?* (PBS), *Short Attention Span Theater* (Comedy Central), *Bugged!* (America's Talking)

JEFF CLINKENBEARD
Supervising Producer's Assistant, *House of Buggin'*
Writers' Assistant, *Cheers* and *Frasier*

JOHN VORHAUS
Writer, *Married With Children, Head of the Class, Charles in Charge,* and *The Flash*
Books: *The Comic Tool Box*

ALAN KIRSCHENBAUM
Co-executive Producer, *Coach*
Co-producer, *Anything but Love*
Created: *Down by the Shore*
Writer, *The New Love American Style* and *Dear John*

JERRY STAHL
Writer, *Moonlighting, Alf, thirtysomething,* and *Twin Peaks*

JON RUBIN
Assistant Manager, Original Comedy Programming, HBO

RICK DORFMAN
Personal Manager, Barry Katz Management

•   •   •

Once after a rather large family dinner, I began obsessing about what direction my writing should take. My cousins and I were gathered in front of the television watching a particularly dismal episode of a marginal sitcom when one cousin asked, "You mean you can't get a job writing *this*?" Now that comment might sound callous, but I took it as a compliment. Television appears to be quite an easy mark to the viewing public and novice writer. After all, we have grown up watching TV, and by virtue of its very familiarity it sure may not look like the product of a creative genius. But when you analyze really successful shows such as *Cheers*, *M*A*S*H*, and *I Love Lucy*, you can appreciate how sophisticated a form it can be.

THE MARKET

With the advent of cable, the number of television channels is increasing exponentially. This has caused concern in the advertising industry, since more choices for the consumer mean less of a stronghold on viewer attention. For the humor writer, however, the wide variety of cable TV channels provides more options to sell work. Certainly the major networks (ABC, NBC, CBS, Fox, Paramount, and Warner Brothers) will remain considerable outlets for sitcoms, game shows, talk shows, sketch comedy shows and comedic films. But there are also lucrative opportunities on the cable channels—MTV, VH-l, HBO, Showtime, Nickelodeon, Cinemax, and Comedy Central, to name a few. What is the difference? As a writer your major concern is *who* is buying the material. Networks, and to some extent cable companies, get their product from outside production companies and syndicators. They also may produce in-house shows as part of their daily programming. You must research which production companies and channels are producing the kind of material you write.

It is important to learn as much about the production end of the business as possible. This will help you understand how humor writing is used and decide the type of show you are most skilled at. Begin by skimming the credits of your favorite shows for listings of production companies.

This is just the first step. In order to learn who the players are, you have to follow the trade magazines such as *The Hollywood Reporter* and *Variety*, and read the industry directories, which are listed in the resources section at the end of this chapter. These publications will give you a sense of who has clout in the industry, which production companies and networks are filming, overall changes in the market that affect the way material is bought, and, most important, who is producing the show that would be the best showcase for your writing. Keeping abreast of industry news also allows you to target your submissions appropriately. This is an important issue, especially if you don't have an agent.

Think of it this way: Does it make sense to submit a sitcom script to a production company that does news shows? It's also a shot in the dark to submit sketch comedy ideas to a company that produces talk shows. The point is to bring your work to the place where it has the best chance of getting read and considered. When you are ready to approach a specific company, call and find out its submission policy as well as the name of the person who reviews submissions. The company may not take material that is not submitted by an agent, although some will agree to read unagented submissions, providing you sign a release form that protects them legally.

When you zero in on a specific company, you can begin to contact people whom you or a friend or a relative know—writers, a production assistant, or somebody's uncle. Submitting to someone in the company guarantees that your material will be read and evaluated.

GETTING STARTED

To prepare for your entry into the network and cable television market, you have to put to use your talent and knowledge of the market. I have broken down the various venues for humor writing into the following categories: sitcoms, talk shows, game shows, and sketch comedy shows.

THE SITCOM

On network television, the sitcom reigns supreme. Recently the field has been dominated by shows built around stand-up comedy performers. *Grace Under Fire, Seinfeld, Roseanne, Ellen, Mad About You,* and *Home Improvement* are successful, which demonstrates how helpful the stand-up connection can be for both performers and writers.

Good writing is still the key, even if a show is stand-up driven. Television sitcom writing calls for more than being able to tell a funny story. It requires:

- A talent for putting a fresh spin on stock situations and established premises.
- An understanding of the sitcom structure.
- An ability to work collaboratively during the writing and pitching process.
- Interpersonal skills to network, work on a team effort basis, and follow through on group assignments.

This may sound like a wish list, especially when you consider how many writers try and fail. Keep in mind that the sitcom business employs up to ten writers per show—that's proof that the wish list is attainable.

Television, like all writing venues, has a certain rhythm. Just knowing you can write doesn't mean television is right for you. You have to evaluate if your skills as a writer match what this market calls for. There's only one way to know. Try it out!

THE SPEC SCRIPT

No one is going to hire you because you're funny or you have a nice idea. They may talk to you, even interview you, but before they give you a job they have to know that you can turn your humor and ideas into a television script.

INSIDE VIEW

"How can anyone tell you if you're good? You have to sit down and write. It's not our job to train. We're looking for established writers."

—GLORIA BANTA

Working on a sample script will help you to clarify what skills you have, which skills you need to develop, and most important, whether you want to focus on sitcom writing. The spec script will also serve as your calling card when you network.

Writing a sample script for a popular show is the perfect starting point. You will not necessarily try to sell the script to the actual show. You'll do this to demonstrate your writing skill and learn the process. Here's how to proceed:

- Watch television. Choose a show with characters and situations you relate to, enjoy, or feel you can write about.
- Analyze the rhythm and timing of the show's humor. This is what you have to duplicate.
- Review the number and types of sets used. A script will seem amateurish if it features too many locations that don't match the show.
- Keep the show's characters in mind. The action usually has to focus on the stars.
- Remember that a sitcom, or any television show for that matter, has an established premise. Your spec script can't change a character or situation in a permanent way. The main character can't move to a new place, have a baby, or die. The *Dallas* shower scene was a fluke.
- If you introduce new characters, they cannot dominate the action permanently or become recurring characters.
- Evaluate the show's structure in its entirety—the timing of the jokes, the way the characters talk and interact with each other, and the way the story unfolds. Your script will have to reflect this structure.

- Integrate the conversations and interactions that normally occur on the show into your story.
- Keep it simple. If your sitcom script looks like it will require a movie budget, you won't look like a savvy writer.
- Your script must be written in the accepted format. The length should be roughly 50–60 pages, and the finished product must be typed on a computer or word processor and printed onto white paper.

When you finish your first spec script, write another one. Most newcomers believe that their first spec script is so great that people should be banging down the doors to hire them. Why? Because they have no perspective. How could they? Stop and think about it. How good are you the first time you do anything? The fact is, you have to grow and learn. This can only be accomplished by repeating the process over and over again.

Perseverance is the key. Its enemies are ego and anxiety. Everyone wants success to happen quickly, but the process of writing script after script will make you a better writer. Growing this way will give you staying power in the business, because it means you have really learned the craft and are not a one-shot wonder. By the time you have written your fourth and fifth scripts you'll be on the road to developing a more discerning eye, which is so crucial for long-term survival in the business. You will also be able to decide if this is how you want to make a living. If you find the process tedious or discover that it doesn't mesh with what you do well, review the other chapters in this book for alternatives.

INSIDE VIEW

"I know one person who pitched ten scripts to a show before he got a job. You can bet the first was nothing like the last. He broke his butt getting better and better. Recognize that at first you are not good enough, and don't get sour about it."

—GLORIA BANTA

Remember that however tough you are on yourself, the industry will be tougher. If you don't persevere, you will fold. Don't let the frustration and rejection overwhelm you. If you aspire to be a television writer, you have to be writing all the time—because you either have an assignment or want to get one. Once you write the best script you can, get someone to read it. And don't be surprised if the criticism is negative, even brutal. Listen to it and keep writing. Decide which part of the critique makes sense to you and work on those aspects of your script. You will improve your writing in stages and become more accustomed to rewriting.

INSIDE VIEW

"We don't start out as good as we think we are, and a lot of the rejections we get early on are well deserved. We have to learn to process rejection in a different way. Take criticism not in terms of how it makes you feel, but rather how it can help your work."

—JOHN VORHAUS

As you continue to improve your overall scriptwriting ability, figure out where your strengths lie, whether it's dialogue, gags, or story lines. You might find work because you fill a niche in a show's writing team. This isn't always the best general approach to landing a job—you certainly don't want to become typecast. But if you hear of a specific opening on a show that would utilize your special skill, use your contacts and capitalize on your expertise.

INSIDE VIEW

"You have to do what you are good at. There are rewrite guys who just pitch jokes, others who are good at putting together a skeleton story line, and some who are great at physical comedy. I've worked with only a few people who were able to write the perfect script. Larry Gelbart and Jim Brooks could do it. It came out of them like Mozart."

—GLORIA BANTA

TALK SHOWS AND GAME SHOWS

The David Letterman show is every comedy writer's dream job. A few lucky writers are given a fax line to submit material to Letterman and Leno. This privilege is reserved for stand-ups who have caught the eye of the show's stars or staff.

Talk shows and game shows are very similar markets. The focus is on short bits that can be incorporated into the show's format. This can include short sketches, funny quiz questions or lists, or monologue material for the host.

INSIDE VIEW

"Talk shows and game shows use comedic bits. It's like stand-up because you have to be short and to the point. As a writer you have to help give the show a different look. On cable television's America's Talking channel, where I work as a writer for the talk show *Bugged!*, I introduced the "Elaine in a Box" character who interacts with an on-line information computer from a box. On *Remote Control*, a game show I worked on at MTV, I not only created characters—to punch up the show's atmosphere—I played them. Comedy bits that click, like the Top Ten List, become part of a show's audience attraction and give it a distinct flavor.

—JOHN TEN EYCK

This material most resembles stand-up joke writing and can be current-events-related or topical. The idea is to do a quick set-up followed by a punch line. To best understand this format, analyze the monologues and other comedy material performed by David Letterman and Jay Leno. Their short-form comedy material includes lists (Letterman's Top Ten List), sketches, pranks (Stupid Pet Tricks), character interviews, parodies, or mock news items (Leno's Headlines feature).

SKETCH COMEDIES

With the success of the Canadian production of *Kids in the Hall*, first seen in the U.S. on HBO, and more recently MTV'S *The State*, ensembles made up of members who write and perform their own material have had wide television exposure. Like their predecessors from *Saturday Night Live*, these performers perfected their sketch comedy writing by working in every venue possible, whether it was the famous Second City Club in Chicago, a school auditorium, or a church basement. My own interest in this form led me to co-found a troupe called OK, SO WE LIED. For five years OK, SO WE LIED appeared regularly at clubs in New York City, colleges, and community organizations. The education I received about developing sketches could not have been duplicated at any school.

Unlike sitcoms, which have built-in premises and characters, sketches have to set up all the vital information in the opening lines and must resolve themselves on a comedic button several minutes later. Although a sketch can be long, as witnessed on *The Tracey Ullman Show*, the format is most effective when kept short. Sketch comedies are generally parodies of commercials, television shows, movies (done especially well on *The Carol Burnett Show*), celebrities, politicians, and music videos (an *In Living Color* favorite). The premises for sketch comedies can also be slice-of-life scenes focusing on relationships people have at home, at the office, or anywhere in the world. The audience must be able to relate to and recognize products, shows, famous people, or familiar situations.

Writing comedy sketches requires creativity. This is a good time to go back to recent comedy history and watch *The Tracey Ullman Show*, *The Carol Burnett Show*, and *In Living Color*, as well as shows from the golden age of television such as *Your Show of Shows*, with Sid Caesar. The sketch writer has the keen sensibility to observe the world around him and twist it into a humorous playlet. This is accomplished by taking the normal everyday aspects of life and adding a comedic edge to them. For example, entering a hotel to register is a routine action, but on *Saturday Night Live*, normal is given a back seat when the registration clerk is John Belushi in his samurai character.

Since it is unlikely that an established ensemble or television show would take on a beginner writer, find a comedy troupe or theater company that will perform your material. These groups are usually making just enough to cover their rent and publicity expenses, so they probably won't be in a position to pay you. This is the trade-off. While you build your portfolio, they get free material. Having your work performed in front of an audience will surprise you. Pieces that you didn't really love will be met with gales of laughter, while other sketches that you thought couldn't miss will elicit a quiet sigh. This is a great opportunity for you to build an audience-tested portfolio. Keep in mind that you should never sign away the rights to pieces for an unpaid performance. If later on the ensemble gets interest from a producer, you will have signed away a possible paycheck. Your material should remain yours until someone likes it enough to pay for it!

CABLE: HOW DOES IT DIFFER FROM NETWORK?

Initially cable competed with network television by offering alternatives—racier comedy, stand-up comedy shows, and youth-oriented programs. These days, cable and network television have a lot in common. For example, Fox's hugely popular *Married With Children* is not a show you would have expected to see on network television a decade ago. As the networks borrow from cable, so does cable take from the networks. The talk show format set by *The Tonight Show* is now being rivaled by talk cable networks. This has been done with a creative twist—just watch *Politically Incorrect* on Comedy Central, on which host Bill Maher and a panel of guests offer comic takes on sensitive, political issues.

The production values and costs of cable programming can vary dramatically. Cable channels offer everything from lavishly produced movies to short, experimental pieces filmed with hand-held cameras. Given this variation, working for a cable station is an easier entrance into the business. The pay is lower, the post- and preproduction time is shorter, and the expectations are different. Since cable channels target specific markets, you need to tailor your work accordingly. Examine the difference between HBO and MTV. Which cable network is the better fit for your work?

INSIDE VIEW

"Fifty percent of our material is acquisitions (e.g.: Monty Python), stand-up, or sketch shows where performers write their own material. I do, however, keep a stash of writers to do alternative forms. I have 1,000 pieces submitted a year but maybe about ten are good enough to be seen or considered. We accept unsolicited material, but most network shows can't because their legal departments would be overrun with complaints. When I was working on *The Mary Tyler Moore Show*, one writer sent a script where Mary had a cold, and said we took his idea. Millions of people have ideas, but it's how it's done."

—GLORIA BANTA

Cable channels accept unsolicited and unagented material more readily than networks. In any case, submitting material is a tricky business, and before you do submit, you should proceed carefully.

- Find out if unsolicited material is accepted. If not, see if you can submit through someone you know at the company, otherwise your script will be dumped unread.
- If unsolicited material is accepted, does a release form need to be signed prior to submitting? Companies will mail these to you. Do yourself a favor—call the receptionist, not the head of production, to find out how to get a release form.
- Cable networks will look at ideas for new shows, something the networks wouldn't consider from a newcomer.
- Lower-budget cable channels are going to look for savvy writers who understand there is no time or money for extensive preproduction and high-priced talent.
- Whenever you submit material to a network, cable station, agent, or production company, enclose a self-addressed, stamped envelope to have your work returned to you. Business is business, and any office receiving hundreds of scripts per week is not going to break the bank returning them.

WRITER/PERFORMERS TAKE NOTE:

HBO has a history of working with comedy performers who establish themselves doing shows featuring their characters. In the quest to find alternatives to network offerings, cable programming executives cruise the comedy clubs and performance spaces. That's how HBO discovered John Leguizamo, and Kathy and Mo and Reno. These performers were diligent enough to develop material, find a performance venue, and network within the industry. Once discovered, performers who are not hired to do their own one-person shows may still get writing gigs for stand-up, sketch, and one-person shows.

INSIDE VIEW

"Regarding comedy, HBO has always been active in developing and associating itself with new talent, including the big three: Whoopi, Robin, and Billy. We pride ourselves on finding the best comedy talent early on. We have a small but extremely active group covering comedy and alternative performers."

—JON RUBIN

COMEDIC FILMS

One cable executive, who preferred to speak off the record, reported that the comedic film has fallen out of favor on both the network and cable airwaves in favor of the sexy thriller or provocative life story. The executive did acknowledge, however, that there is always a market for a truly funny comedy film. To sell scripts, writers should approach production companies that produce these films independently for both network and cable television as well as film companies.

EDUCATION AND TRAINING

Even the most renowned writing school can't promise that you will find work. If you do choose to go to a college or school for television arts, select one that offers intern programs. This is on-the-job training that will give you experience, a credit for your resume, and a chance to build relationships with people in the industry.

INSIDE VIEW

"UCLA, USC, NYU, The Academy of Television Arts and Sciences, and even your local continuing education class can be good places to learn beginning scripts. If you go to one of these classes and there's no discussion of structure, it's a bad class. In sitcom format, structure is everything. It's not enough to write a funny script; you have to write in the conventional style that fits the format."

—ALAN KIRSCHENBAUM

There are certain core ideas that classroom training should focus on. They are as follows:

Structure

The television sitcom script has its own specific structure that differs greatly from that of a film script or a play. Understanding structure means synthesizing all the aspects of the sitcom format: timing, character relationships, situations, and settings. If you are going to take a class, evaluate how structure is emphasized and explained. Is it presented in a concrete, learnable manner? If not, consider looking for a different class.

INSIDE VIEW

"People deny the importance of structure because they don't understand it. They then assume it's not important. I learned about structure in a lot of different classes that taught it, but I didn't understand it. Not because they were bad teachers or because I was stupid. We just didn't speak the same language. So I had to teach myself structure in a language that I did understand. I looked at the parts of structure I didn't understand and broke them down until I did."

—JOHN VORHAUS

A good class in structure will teach you how to write a script in sitcom format. Refer to your class notes while watching sitcoms. Observe the theory in practice. Mimic writing the pieces you're watching. If you have difficulty learning the basics of structure in class, put more time in on your own. Eventually you will either grasp sitcom structure or discover that this style of writing is not for you. Either way you can move on. Good luck!

Feedback

Writing is a solitary act—marketing your work to the public is not. A good class should offer you an opportunity to have your work read and evaluated by the teacher and other students. This is crucial. A class where your work is not reviewed is not going to help you hone your comic voice. In addition, you have to consider the nature of the feedback. If it's bombastic and unconstructive and discourages you from working, then the class is counterproductive.

INSIDE VIEW

"If you don't like the teacher, their point of view, or if they don't offer strong criticism that promotes better writing on your part, move on."

—JON RUBIN

Having performed my writing in front of an audience, I understand the value of constructive feedback. If you are not part of a class, invite people to your home and read and listen to your work. Tape-record or video-tape the process and study the results. Feedback is less brutal when you see it as a necessary part of the learning process.

Comedy History

You need to look back into comic history for successful examples of how theory is put into practice. Even professionals know enough to value what has come before them. A friend who works at New York's Museum of Broadcasting often tells me of the famous performers and writers who come regularly to view the collection. Old shows are invaluable resources when it comes to understanding the presentation of humor, timing, and setting up premises. They also show you the options that exist within the sitcom or sketch formats. These shows can be inspirational if you can take a fresh approach to the elements used. If a trip to the museum is not a possibility for you, your local library, video stores, and cable television stations are packed with vintage shows. Don't limit your research to the comedy history of television. Reviewing Neil Simon's plays, Billy Wilder's films, or the comic pieces of *any* medium can be an eye-opener.

WORKSHOPS, CONFERENCES, SEMINARS, AND WRITING PROGRAMS

Much can be learned about the television industry in workshops, conferences, seminars, and writing programs. If you read the trades, you should have no problem finding out about specific events. Be sure to attend those functions run by lecturers who are active in the business. Television has changed too much in recent years for you to get useful information from someone who hasn't worked in decades. Just by attending you may add to your network of connections. Talk to the other attendees and look for opportunities to meet the presenters.

INSIDE VIEW

"Read Molière, Shaw, and the classic plays. Basically we're still doing the same things. For example in Sheridan's *The Rivals* there is a character, Mrs. Malaprop. She misuses words and concepts, hence the expression malapropism. We have this character in television today. The characters of Woody and Coach on *Cheers* illustrate this best."

—JEFF CLINKENBEARD

Jon Rubin landed his job at HBO after meeting a vice president of original programming at the Warner Brothers writing program. The executive liked Rubin's sensibilities and hired him. How did he get into the writing program in the first place? He did some research. HBO, Disney, and The Children's Television Workshop offer similar writing programs but don't always publicize them in the general press. The hardest part is finding out that they exist. So how do you apply? You have to read the trades, network, or get information from whatever reliable source is available to you. What the programs are looking for varies depending on the needs of the company. Through writing programs, companies can train and evaluate new writers to work in a specific style, develop new voices, and find undiscovered talent.

BREAKING IN

There is no one right way to break into the business; just about anything goes! If you talk with successful people in the industry, you will find that very few of them followed a traditional path. Getting a writing assignment will be the truest test of your creativity.

Here are some tips that can help you put yourself where the action is:

- Work in some other area of television, and find out which person within the company you should submit your work to.
- Capitalize on your special skills. Consider working in the business as a secretary, production assistant or an entry-level gofer.
- Exploit the theory of "six degrees of separation." Do your friends and family know anyone in a position to help you network and get your work seen?

- Develop and maintain relationships with people in the industry.
- Get your work out there in other media to show outside validation—comedy clubs, radio or periodicals.
- Be nice! Save your "difficult period" until you're so valuable that people will have to tolerate you.

INSIDE VIEW

"Anyone who's good doesn't need to go to a professional seminar because they find a way through their intelligence to network and get in as either a production assistant or some other job. I remember taking typing because I knew I could be a secretary. I went around to ABC, CBS, NBC and took typing tests. I was sent in to work with the writers. I listened to the writers pitch and soon I began pitching. You have to be exposed to everything and come through the ranks to really know the business. Read the trades to know everything that's going on, who's doing what and where. It's easy today because show business is overexposed: It's in your face constantly. You should look at who's producing the shows you feel something for and try to work or submit material to that producer or production company."

—GLORIA BANTA

EXPOSURE: WORKING WITHIN THE TELEVISION MEDIUM

The television industry operates like any other manufacturing concern. That means there are a variety of people employed in different jobs. As a beginner, you might not be hired to write, but there are other ways to get into the game. Once you've landed a job, keep writing. When you're ready, show your work to the contacts you've made within the company.

You can make yourself an asset to any aspect of the production process of a television show. Writers, producers, stars, and directors need secretaries and personal assistants. Production crews need gofers to do everything from carrying equipment to buying lunch. If you have good organizational or clerical skills, you may be able to secure an entry-level position, which will allow you to network with insiders and learn more about the business.

NETWORKING

Your script will never find a home if you don't meet people who are working in the business. You have to make and nurture contacts in the places where industry people mingle. Through networking, I was able to get my work directly to production companies without an agent. On one occasion, an actress studying in the improvisation class I was teaching did a guest spot on a sitcom. She told the producers how funny she thought I was, and they agreed to see a script. On another occasion, a fellow student in an acting class recommended me to a producer he had grown up with.

INSIDE VIEW

"Friendships can be a definite doorway. I was spotted hanging out at Catch A Rising Star by a schoolmate from Emerson College. The friend, now a vice president at MTV, asked me if I still wrote. He remembered me from the comedy workshop at college and thought I was funny. He invited me to pitch. I did, and began working on *Remote Control*. This was a break I was ready for because I had continued to perform and develop my writing for a decade after college."

—JOHN TEN EYCK

I can tell you one sure way how *not* to network. I was at a party watching this guy talk to people. Whenever he slithered up to someone he thought could help him, he handed them several copies of his scripts. Needless to say, he didn't impress anyone. And when the guests departed, they left behind the scripts. It's fine to try to connect with others at parties or events, but you have to let relationships evolve. It's best to meet people on a casual basis. They'll be more helpful if they like you, think you're smart and funny, or feel you have something to offer.

INSIDE VIEW

"I wrote a short story for *Playboy* about a dentist who ran away from home because he missed the sixties and wanted to have a good time. He winds up in a van with a mohawk haircut and a 15-year-old girl. A producer of *Alf* was so taken with the story he hired me to write for the show even though I had no idea how to write a sitcom script. I didn't even know how many pages a script should be. I was clueless, so I spoke to some guys I knew who worked for TV. They were appalled and told me a script was 100 pages. I found out later it was more like 50 pages. My weaknesses were overcome by my strengths. I could always write funny dialogue. This kept me working. The producer stood by me, and amazingly I failed upwards. I got an agent at CAA (Creative Artists Agency) through an old girlfriend. CAA hooked me up to *Moonlighting,* where my ability to write funny dialogue really paid off."

—JERRY STAHL

INSIDE VIEW

"Be aware of what you can do for someone else, because in the beginning no one can do anything for you. My mother made me take shorthand and attend business school because she knew I wasn't going to take a conventional track and she wanted me to have skills. She was right. It was my way in. Learning about the business helped me to focus on what I could do. Since sitcom writers sit in rooms mouthing off ideas to one another at 100 miles a minute, they need someone to take notes. I sent a mailing to every television sitcom production with a first line that read 'I TAKE SHORTHAND AT 90 WPM.' A week later I landed a job on the short-lived *Good and Evil*; two weeks later I was working on *Cheers*. Stick with your friends. Make their successes your successes. Keep in touch with people. I did with the people I met in acting, improv, and on creative projects. You just pick up the phone and say, 'What's going on?' Relationships are the nature of the business, and you never work with one person for very long. In this fashion the people you worked with will be a source of information or referral, or will even be able to hire you."

—JEFF CLINKENBEARD

OUTSIDE VALIDATION

Hollywood loves outside validation. If you have been successful in other areas, people will take you seriously and see your work. When querying an agent, always highlight your published or performed work. If you've been published in a mainstream way or have had your material performed on the radio or stage, you'll make a serious impression.

GOING IN COLD

Some writers have no alternative but to resort to the cold call. I can only recommend cold calling when there are no other options available. It's risky and requires finesse. If you are going to try cold calling or a query letter, keep this in mind: If you were receiving tons of messages every day, would you return a message from a total stranger? When you do make contact through a cold call, make sure that you are completely familiar with the kind of work that production company does. Producers and production companies aren't clearing houses. Any material that doesn't fit their needs is considered junk mail. So guess where it ends up? Once in a while a producer gets a script he or she loves but can't use and may then offer to help that writer, but this is a pretty unlikely scenario.

INSIDE VIEW

"There are people whose job it is to tell disen-
franchised writers not to send their scripts. It
doesn't mean you can't do it. I did and my strategy paid off. It never hurts for people to think
well of you. Every phone call can help you if you
make a good-faith offer and not come across as
an adversary or needy person. I used to spend
my day beating my head against the phone until
I got people to take my submissions. Then I
waited and kept writing to get better and have
something new to show because you never know
when someone will want to see more. This phe-
nomenon of Hollywood is known as the black
hole of spec scripts. Sometimes your script will
just disappear and never get read. You then have
a choice. Do you wait and bitch and moan or do
you have a career? I came to L.A. with one contact name, a friend who had made it in the business. He taught me, helped me write my first
spec script, and was my mentor, because he
knew I was willing to work."

—JOHN VORHAUS

Your reputation as a writer can be a major consideration to others when you're starting out. But how can
they really evaluate you before you have major writing
credits? When you have a repertoire of good material,

people get a strong sense that you will work hard and have many ideas. This perception is crucial. After all, a producer has to turn out a season of shows that will be rewritten dozens of times before filming.

PITCHING

Even if a producer sees your work and believes it shows merit, the material may not reflect exactly what he or she is looking for. You may, however, be invited to pitch ideas that are more suitable. Pitching is the process during which a writer meets with a show's staff and producers to present story ideas. There is a certain element of performance involved in pitching, and it's a skill that is essential to the development of your career as a writer.

Before your meeting, you should find out as much as you can about the company and the people to whom you are pitching. If you have friends in the business who have already pitched to them or know them, ask about the kinds of projects they do and what the sessions were like. If you have been following the trades and watching television, you will already have an idea of what they have worked on. The more you learn about the show's style, pacing, content, and characters, the better your chances of landing a job. Watch the show as much as possible. This is especially easy if the show is in syndicated reruns. Poll your friends to see if any of them are over-the-top fans of that show. Review your ideas carefully to see if they have been used already.

Inside View

"Having been in the position of both pitching and being pitched to, my best advice is to go in with a lot of story ideas that you have practiced pitching prior to the meeting. Know how to tell your story succinctly. I've seen people go on and on, and even if I politely let them, it's still no sale. A professional writer can get the story premise fairly quickly. If someone is talking for three or four minutes describing the first scene, I can generally tell if I'm interested or if it will work for the show I'm doing. In general, you won't sell your first idea. It may be an idea you really love, but they'll say they don't like it or we've done it. Don't argue; go on to your next idea. You should have six or seven. Chances are that the idea they'll like is the one you thought of on the way to the meeting which you haven't worked out. It's Murphy's Law. Even if you don't make a sale, you'll gain experience and be better at it the next time. In any case, listen to the criticism.

To prepare, the best thing to do is watch the show. If it's really good, someone on the show knows what they are doing. If the show's not good, you still want to sell them a script, but not necessarily use their criticism. Remember to be confident, but don't be cocky. If you're going to pitch for a show that you think is bad, don't think that the people who work

> there think it's a bad show. Some people really care about the shows they do, and think highly of their work even if you don't."
>
> —ALAN KIRSCHENBAUM

Most important, you should understand what the project is. In a casual meeting with a producer, writer John Ten Eyck pitched a series of five-minute comedic bits only to learn the show was looking for half-hour spots. In retrospect he realized he should have clarified the format of the show prior to his meeting.

The first few times you pitch will be learning experiences. Remember, you're pitching comedy material. Have energy, express yourself clearly, demonstrate your wit when possible. And of course, show that you have confidence.

As if the whole idea of pitching isn't intimidating enough, you may find yourself pitching to ten people. You have to be prepared. If you don't have a performance background, it's important to be organized. A standard trick is to outline your ideas on index cards and arrange them in the order you want to offer them.

The very nature of pitching requires being sharp enough to be able to size up the situation. Someone with years of experience as a performer can work a room easily. Most writers will not be able to do this without practice. Prepare for pitch sessions by experimenting with stand-up, improvisation, or even sales classes. Try pitching to a

---

Inside View

"Just like writers aren't salesmen, they aren't pitchmen either. The point of a pitch is to make a sale. If the producers like an idea, they'll pay you to write the story, but you have to be able to pitch it. I believe in taking responsibility for your gift. A lot of writers feel like they have to excuse themselves. With writing your ego is on the line, so you build up excuses for a gentle let-down. For example: *I know you won't like this, but* . . . Not only is this unhealthy, it's unproductive, because if you don't like your work, how do you expect other people to? You have to be at the top of your energy so even if they don't buy anything, they'll think of you favorably."

—JOHN VORHAUS

---

group of friends in your living room. You need to get used to presenting your ideas verbally and being ready to move on when told, even if it's in the middle of a story outline.

One crucial piece of advice is something I heard over and over again from industry insiders. The trick is to pitch after lunch. The last thing you want is to face a room full of hungry people who are waiting for you to finish. If you are given a choice of appointments, try to get an early morning or late afternoon slot. Also consider which of the times of the day are best for you. Keep in mind, however, that these appointments are hard to come by. If you are given a time near lunch, take it anyway. You may not get another chance. Go in prepared, organized, and rehearsed. Once in the office, be sure to remain focused. Listen carefully and respond diplomatically to questions and comments. This meeting should not be about arguing. It should be about the beginning of a relationship. Even if there is no sale, you might want an opportunity to pitch to this group of people again.

SUBMITTING YOUR WORK

Whenever you have the opportunity to submit your work, consider the following steps:

- Call and find out the submission policy. The company may accept only agented material, require that you are recommended by someone they know, or have you fill out a release form. Any assistant or secretary can usually relay this information.
- Send a query letter about your work. Do not send a manuscript unless one is requested. The query should contain a brief but interesting description of the completed work. It should also explain why you're sending your work to that particular person and/or production company. For example, you might mention that you have a special interest in the kinds of shows the company produces. Add to the query letter anything that makes you stand out—awards, high-profile publications, or grants that you may have received.

- When asked to submit material, send along a self-addressed stamped envelope for your work to be returned. For your protection, it is wise to register the script with the Writers Guild or the Library of Congress. See Appendix IV for more information.
- If you use the Postal Service, send the script by certified mail. This way you will know if it has been received. If you do not receive a response within two to three weeks, call and ask politely if your script has been reviewed yet. While you are waiting for a verdict, *write*!

PAYMENT

This is where the difference between cable and network television becomes obvious. In general, networks pay more for material and offer residuals. Also keep in mind that the money varies depending on whether the job is nonunion or covered by the Writers Guild contract. You will be apprised of payments prior to signing any contracts. Even if you don't have an agent, you may want to review the offer with one before making a commitment.

RESOURCES

Trade Magazines and Directories
The Gale Directory of Publications and Broadcast Media.
Gale Research, Inc., 835 Penobscot Bldg., Detroit MI

48226-4094. Available at most libraries, this annual guide highlights network television and cable stations among its media listings.

Hollywood Creative Directory. 3000 Olympic Blvd., Santa Monica CA 90404. Tel: 310-315-4815. This company produces several directories that list production companies, representation possibilities, and other resources.

Daily Variety and *Weekly Variety*. 5700 Wilshire Blvd., Suite 120, Los Angeles CA 90036. Tel: 213-857-6600. Industry news in all fields of entertainment. *Daily Variety* features an updated list of production companies and their current and upcoming projects.

The Hollywood Reporter. 5055 Wilshire Blvd., Los Angeles CA 90036. Tel: 213-525-2000. Insider industry news and a listing of production companies. There is both a weekly and daily edition.

Backstage. Subscriber Services and Information, P.O. Box 5017, Brentwood TN 37024. Tel: 615-377-3322. An information weekly that spotlights different areas of the entertainment industry.

Television Index, Inc. 40-29 27th St., Long Island City NY 11101. Tel: 718-937-3990. Television Index Information Services: This company offers a variety of weekly reports and a semiannual index of listings of production companies and agents. Titles include *Television Index* (weekly), *TV Pro-Log* (weekly), *Network Futures* (weekly), *Ross Reports Radio-TV Contact Service* (quarterly), *Ross Reports Television* (monthly), *Ross Reports USA* (quarterly), *Television Index Annual* (annual), and *Writers Directory/Production Register* (annual).

Catalogs

Script City. Tel: 800-676-2522. Offers thousands of movie and television scripts, as well as books, seminars on tape, and writer's software.

Book City. Tel: 800-4-CINEMA. Carries a large selection of screenplays and movie books.

Samuel French, Inc. 7623 West Sunset Blvd., Hollywood CA 90046. Tel: 213-876-0570. Publishes reference and how-to books dealing with all aspects of the film industry.

The Drama Bookshop. 723 7th Avenue, New York NY 10019. Tel: 212-944-0595 or 800-322-0595. Offers a large selection of books about television, film and theater.

Books

The Hollywood Reporter Yearly Blue Book. $59.95 plus $4.95 for shipping. Blue Book Orders, Circulation Dept., 5055 Wilshire Blvd., Los Angeles CA 90036. Tel: 213-525-2150. A film, TV, and video directory.

The Elements of Screenwriting by Irwin R. Blacker. $5.95. Collier Books, Macmillan Publishing Co., 866 3rd Ave., New York NY 10022.

Hollywood Creative Directory Guide to Producers, Studios, Network Executives, and Production Companies. $45.00. Hollywood Creative Directory, 3000 Olympic Blvd., Suite 2525, Santa Monica, CA 90404. Tel: 310-315-4815.

Successful Sitcom Writing by Jergen Wolff. $17.95. St. Martin's Press, 175 5th Avenue, New York NY 10010.

Television and Screenwriting from Concept to Contract by Richard A. Blum. $26.95. Focal Press, Butterworth-Heineman, 313 Washington St., Newton MA 02158-1626.

How to Write for Television: How to Write Treatments, Pilots, Sitcoms, Hour-long Dramas, TV Movies by Madeline Dimaggio. $12.00. A Fireside book. Simon & Schuster, 1230 Avenue of the Americas, New York NY 10020.

How to Make It in Hollywood—Everything you need to know about agents, managers, lawyers, chutzpa, schmoozing, the casting couch, the Godfather call, rhino skin, handling rejection, how to be lucky and all the steps you need to achieve the success you deserve by Linda Buzzell. $11.00. A Harper Perennial. HarperCollins Publishers, 10 E. 53rd St., New York NY 10022.

Organizations

The Writers Guild of America. East Tel: 212-767-7800; West Tel: 310-550-1000. This organization offers registration services to protect your work. For members, it supplies industry practice and payment standards for contracts and negotiations, writing fellowships, symposiums, panel discussions, and awards programs. Call for details and membership criteria. The Writers Guild East covers writers who live east of the Mississippi. Writers living west of the Mississippi are covered by the Writers Guild West.

The Writers Network. 289 South Robertson Blvd., Suite 465, Beverly Hills CA 90211. Tel: 310-275-0287. A growing organization created by writers. Features a newsletter, seminars, and services to help writers improve their work and find producers. This is an extremely helpful organization, especially for new writers.

Chapter 3

Film:

The Hollywood Dream Factory

THE MOVIE MOGULS

LEN AMATO
Vice President, East Coast Development and Spring Creek
Productions

LEW HUNTER
Writer: *Fallen Angel, Playing with Fire, If Tomorrow Comes*
Program Executive, ABC, CBS, and NBC
Story Executive, Disney, Hanna-Barbera
Author: *Lew Hunter's Screenwriting 434*

AUDREY KELLY
Managing Director, The Writers Network

JENNY RAUCHER
Story Editor, Scott Rubin Productions

MARK MILLER
Writer (film): *Home by Midnight;* (TV): *Different Strokes, The
Carol Burnett Show, The Jeffersons, The Facts of Life*
Author: *Los Angeles Times* humor column

MARTY WALDMAN
Press Representative, Writers Guild of America East

• • •

From the brilliance of Billy Wilder's *Some Like It Hot* to the high-concept movie *Big*, there is no experience equal to laughing out loud with hundreds of people at a well-written screen comedy. Mastering the art of screenwriting means being able to take the audience out of its everyday existence into the realm of a visually told story that is larger than life.

It's no wonder so many writers are drawn to film work. And if it's your passion to write a screenplay, you should not be deterred. Every great film starts in the same place a new writer does—with a blank page. But proceed with caution. We've all heard the Hollywood horror stories of double-dealing, films never being made, and writers earning nothing on a film that earns the production company and the studio hundreds of millions of dollars. The trick is to keep your passion and your wits about you to survive in the business and grow as a writer.

THE MARKET

Movie studios, production companies, independent producers, directors, stars, agents, and distribution companies all play a part in the creation of a film. Add to this the fact that even a small film can cost millions of dollars, and you see how complicated the process can be.

Your job as a writer, however, remains constant. Write the best film possible and get people with clout to read it!

Production companies all have one thing in common—they need new material. Independent film makers were once associated with small-budget horror movies, art films, or offbeat movies. While for some companies this still holds true, the overall description no longer applies. Miramax and New Line Cinema, for example, operate more like large movie studios than tiny homegrown movie companies. And it's not necessarily easier to get material read by independents. You have to know the people involved.

Studio Executives: They develop and green-light film production. They may, for financial reasons, oversee the budget and production.

Executive Producer: The financial captain of the project.

Producer: The producer may also develop a film from a script or other medium and put together a collaborative team of directors, actors, and design people.

Director: Transforms the script into a story told in the visual medium.

Development People: Studio executives who scour books, plays, magazine articles, newspaper pieces, short stories, and scripts looking for material that fits their studio's agenda.

Scouts: Employees of production and development companies whose job it is to find material for potential films before anyone else.

Readers: Employees of production or development companies who read scripts, plays, books, and other source material and provide what is called a "coverage report." This report evaluates whether the material could be made into a film.

Agents/Personal Managers: The liaison between actors and directors, screenwriters and production companies. They may package a writer/director/star deal or act as advocates for their clients.

These titles and profiles are not written in stone. Although one person might be given a specific title, he may actually perform any of the various roles described above. Your script may start and end with any of these people.

Several professionals have told me they have more to read than they can possibly get to. They go through a process of elimination. A script is tossed immediately if it's not in script format, if the first page doesn't grab them, if the synopsis is trite or unclear, if the script is too thick or too thin, and so on. Don't be deterred by this information; you can use it to your advantage. If you are an unknown, but your script is clean, formatted, and sparkles with wit, you have a chance of having the material read in its entirety. This is what you want most.

To maintain an ongoing sense of the market and the people involved, it is important to read the industry trades: *The Hollywood Reporter* and *Variety*.

GETTING STARTED

As always, the most important writer's affirmation is "Write, write, write and perfect your craft." And to best understand how to write a screenplay, you actually have to do it.

THE SPEC SCRIPT

The spec script is an uncommissioned full-length feature that you write. This is different from writing on spec, which I will review later in the chapter. The point of writing the spec script is:

- To learn the craft of screenwriting.
- To begin a body of work so you have material to submit.
- To assess if the medium is right for you.

What will set you apart is *your own voice*. This is all about you! Although the comedy genre includes formula films, TV-based films, and sequels, these are not going to reflect the originality of your talent. And believe me, if professionals are reading dozens of scripts, a fresh idea will hold their interest. It's also important to note that sequel or TV-based film scripts will be complicated for a film company to consider because other studios or individuals may actually own the rights.

INSIDE VIEW

"In the Ecclesiasticus section of the Bible, it is written that everything has been done before. What is unique is your particular viewpoint. A person's particular interpretation of a story brings their own needs, energy, passion, and problems to the script."

—LEW HUNTER

A buzzword that is often used is "high-concept." This can be a confusing term, and it's not always an absolute. The term "high-concept" refers to an idea that, when presented, immediately explains itself. It tells something about the action, plot, and character in just one sentence.

When selecting your theme, it is important to choose wisely. You have to create high stakes—something must happen that will hook an audience. By the end of the film a big change in the lives of the characters needs to take place. The main characters must be sympathetic, whether it's because they're struggling, fighting, or enduring. The audience has to care about these characters. The resolution has to be strong. Nobody is going to want to finish reading your script (or, if you're lucky, watch your film) and feel disappointed. This doesn't always hold true for dramatic films that often depict the tragedy of life or circumstance. But a comedy should make people leave with a smile. In the hugely successful *Dumb and Dumber*, the two main characters are no better off in the end. Yet this is acceptable to the audience because it's handled in a funny way and the characters remain incredibly appealing. Their naivete (or stupidity) is part of the fun.

Earlier I said that all films start the same way—with a blank page. In the beginning this piece of paper looks immense. Your job of completing a spec script will be easier if you break down the task into smaller parts. First, write a couple of sentences that explain your plot. Jot down sentences that describe the beginning, the middle and the end of your story. Build an outline around those points. Continue to embellish until the outline resembles a short story. Keep adding until the characters, action, conflict, and resolution are completely fleshed out. Break down this story line into three acts and write it in script format. Take a break after you finish, then go back and polish the dialogue. Raise the stakes and clarify the action. In short, screenwriting requires that you follow the writer's adage—"Writing is rewriting."

Remember that film is a visual medium, and your script should tell the story in pictures. This does not mean you need to worry slavishly about camera angles. Those are integrated into the shooting script, which is composed by the director and/or production company. Your job is to tell the story.

When the script is finished, start a new one. Writing constantly is the best way to learn the craft of screenwriting. People can advise you and even help you improve, but only through repetition will you hone your skill, and that's your first priority. When your script is finished, evaluate it in the following ways:

Does the script tell the story completely?

Does the script provide all the information a reader needs to follow the plot as it unfolds? If there is any confusion, it means that you are missing a piece of your story puzzle or, as they say in the business, your "beat." Decide which "beat" (information or scenes) is missing and add accordingly.

Does the script have scenes that don't propel the story forward? A hysterically funny bit that's not incorporated into the story will slow down the reader. You must be merciless here. Sometimes great stuff will have to go. Learn to lose even your favorite parts if they interfere with or delay your story in a meaningless way. One comedic moment should not control your whole script.

Is the story told chronologically?

Even if flashbacks are used, every scene should propel the action along logically. A flashback should highlight something, explain a character motivation, or outline a prior experience. When you're first writing a script, you may insert scenes that interfere with the order. This process may help to guide you as you create plot or character motivation, but these scenes may not be appropriate for the final draft. Any scene should integrate itself organically and push the story ahead.

To help you with this process, there are a number of screenwriting handbooks you can review and workshops you can attend. These are listed in the Resources section at the end of this chapter. I would recommend glancing at several screenwriting books to get a feel for the technique involved. This will give you the opportunity to find a teaching style you can understand and identify with.

WRITING ON SPEC

You write on spec to learn your craft and develop your portfolio. Of course, your ultimate goal is selling your work. If a producer commissions you to write a script on spec, this is a different scenario, especially if you sign away rights to the finished work. In my own experience this has never worked out. I have found consistently that deals are legitimate from day one, and a person who can get the money to produce a film should be able to get money to pay you. This is what a producer does. Think of it this way: If your script is good enough for someone else to get backing for it, you'll find a place to sell it yourself. I firmly believe that. Still, for many writers, going into a spec situation with a producer has been a doorway into the business. If you do so, the only thing you should count on is getting writing experience and an addition to your portfolio.

Even if you are promised a deferred payment, it doesn't mean you'll see a dime. Get any agreement in writing, and be sure to keep all the rights unless you are paid for them. Have contracts reviewed by an independent attorney to make sure your rights are protected. In addition, review Appendix IV at the end of the book to learn where to find free legal advice.

No established producer who is a signatory to the Writers Guild of America can legitimately ask you to write for free. You should inquire at either the Writers Guild of America East or West (refer to the Resources section at the end of this chapter) to see if the producer you are dealing with is a member. There are, however, a number of independent producers who are not Writers Guild members. Check them out any way possible. If you have been active in developing a network of contacts in the business, call them. Ask the producer which companies he has worked for and whom he's worked with. Call these referrals. If he's that new or unconnected he certainly won't be able to get a project going based on clout, only on chutzpa.

It could happen if the project you've been commissioned to write has real appeal. If, however, the script the producer wants you to write is so specific it won't be of any interest to anyone else, think about the nature of the project. If the producer who commissioned your script decides not to buy it, would it be a viable project at another company?

INSIDE VIEW

"Write on spec for a producer only if it's yours when it's done and you can sell it elsewhere and/or it's something you want to write. But if it's something specific like *Lesbian Invaders from Mars,* that no one else would want, you may be wasting your time."

—MARK MILLER

EDUCATION AND TRAINING

As with any art form, there are formal (schools, workshops, and seminars) and informal (reading, watching films, and visiting museums) ways to improve your craft.

In the case of screenwriting, a combination of both will not only offer you instruction but motivation and inspiration.

INFORMAL TRAINING

Screenwriting is still storytelling and anything that helps you recognize the mechanics of a good story will be helpful. Reading classic novels or the literary short stories in *The New Yorker* and *Story* magazine will demonstrate the importance of structure, character, and individual style. The aspiring screenwriter should also be watching films all the time. Analyze how other writers have used the visual medium to propel the plot of their stories. It is also important to read film scripts. These are available in libraries (especially those with performing arts branches), in stores, and through catalog services (see the Resources section at the end of the chapter). Evaluate how other writers present their stories on the page. Also, it's a great exercise to read a screenplay and watch the film simultaneously. With a VCR and a wide selection of films on video at your fingertips, it should be easy to explore how words translate into film.

I also recommend visiting museums and galleries. Exciting visual imagery manifests itself in many forms—whether it's in paintings by the great masters and conceptual artists or in designs in architecture. Learning about eye-catching imagery can only help you develop as a screenwriter.

FORMAL TRAINING

Going to a film school will certainly give you an impressive credential and the chance to network. But as a writer, you simply need a class that will help develop your sense of plot, character, and dialogue. There are a variety of screenwriting programs that focus on good writing as opposed to film studies. You should review the faculty profiles. Does their work demonstrate that they are great storytellers? Is the school attracting students who go on to become successful screenwriters? Does the school have internships through which you can work for film production companies? A school that satisfies this criteria will offer you networking possibilities through alumni organizations and industry exposure.

Conferences, seminars, and workshops will also improve your writing and give you insight into the business as a whole. When you read the trades, keep tabs on upcoming opportunities. Review Appendix II at the end of the book for more information on this subject.

INSIDE VIEW

"If you want to write novels, you read novels. So it's only natural that if you want to write film, you have to read scripts. Structure is so important. A script is a blueprint. There's a linear quality to movies that has to be maintained."

—LEN AMATO

NETWORKING

Earlier in the chapter, I stressed that every screenwriter has two jobs: Write the best movie and get it read. To some, writing a great movie may actually seem easier than getting it read. But it's entirely possible to get your script to the right person or production company, particularly if you use a bit of creativity.

Writer's Affirmation: Six Degrees of Separation

Poll everyone you know for contacts in the film business and have them ask everyone they know for suggestions. You're looking for anyone who works at an agency or production company. This may seem far-fetched, but using someone's name can often put you on top of the heap. Getting your work read doesn't mean that your work will be bought. Your work will have to sell itself.

GET INVOLVED

If you're not living in Los Angeles or New York, then it's not possible to be where the action is. If filmmaking does go on where you live, try to get a job as a production assistant.

Conferences, workshops, and seminars can also hook you up to industry players. Select programs that allow you direct access to speakers. Many conferences offer informal cocktail hours; others seat speakers with you at lunch. If you do have the chance to talk to industry people in these settings, do not pull out your script. Talk to them about the business, their ideas, specific writers they admire. Use this information to pitch them later in a query letter in which you ask them to read your work.

Correspond with writers, agents, directors, or producers about their work. Point out something they have said or done that you feel is critical to the art of filmmaking and helpful to your work. Sometimes an intellectual discussion will pique their interest. In a best-case scenario, they will write back and ask you about your work.

COLD CALL

Reading the trades and networking can help you figure out who's doing what in the business. The key here is professionalism. Call a production company or agent's office and ask the receptionist for the submission policy. They may advise you to procure and sign a release form or submit a query letter. The query should include a synopsis of your script and any other relevant bits of information that explain why you wish to send your script to them. Be specific about why your work is in keeping with their company's projects, or mention, if it's appropriate, that you've read that they work well with new writers, etc. If you can't come up with a good reason to pitch your work to them, it may not be the right place. A comedy script won't be taken seriously at a production company that does only horror films. Focus your energy where it makes sense. Now for the hard part. The query should be as brief as possible—certainly no longer than a page. This letter also has to show that you can tell a story in synopsis form. You have to be as creative with this query as with your script. It's your calling card.

INSIDE VIEW

"It's tough when you don't have an agent, you don't want to seem glib, but you do want to catch the eye of the person you're submitting to. The best tool is a good cover letter. You should not just send a script. Most places won't look at unsolicited material, and studios even discourage employees from reading material from an agent they don't know due to possible lawsuits. Immersing yourself in writing will help you find people who will look at your work. There are smaller development companies that nurture new writers or new fledgling agents. Robert McKee's screenwriting classes are great because you learn structure, and industry people attend, so you can network. Film festivals are helpful for seeing what's out there, and you should read the trades to see who's buying stuff in a particular vein. If you are writing in a similar style, express that. It's better than a bland submission."

—AUDREY KELLY

HANG OUT

You'll find opportunities to forge connections if you live in an area where industry people eat, drink, volunteer, or even work out. Nurture these friendships. If real bonds grow, these people will help you. And even if they can't help you directly, they may offer valuable insight into the people you need to contact and the way the industry works.

AGENTS

When you have no writing credits, anyone who will get your work read is a godsend. If possible, however, submit your work to a number of agencies and while you wait for a response, understand the differences between large and small agencies.

Smaller agencies will usually work harder for beginner clients. Being smaller doesn't mean they're not well connected. An independent agency that has spun off from a large company with an established history might have excellent contacts. If, however, the agency is small because it is new to the business, realize it will take longer to get your material read.

If you submit to larger agencies, there's a chance that your work will get lost in the dreaded slush pile. I can't say this is always the case—I've known many people who have cold called, sent a query, then a script, and gotten representation at a huge, powerful agency. Big agencies can be particularly helpful in that they package deals for studios. A newcomer's script paired with a hot actor and/or a director will give a project extra appeal. You will go through a few agents over the course of your writing life. Remember, this is Hollywood and it's not always a pleasant journey.

Key points to consider when you sign with an agent:

- Don't sign a long-term contract. If the agent is getting you work and treating you well, why would you move on? The agent should work to keep you just as you should work to keep the agent. Many big agencies work with writers on a noncontractual basis.
- Have everything reviewed by your own attorney. Don't believe that your agent always has your best interests in mind. The law is complicated and ever-changing—you want to make sure you have the final word.
- Give up as little control as possible. Every so often, ask where your work is being submitted. Call or fax with leads or suggestions. And, whenever possible, have your money paid directly to you.

The real irony is that to secure an agent who will get you work in the future, first you may have to get work on your own. If a producer expresses interest in your work and makes you an offer, call the agent or agency you most want to work with and ask them to negotiate for you. The producer will understand your need to have someone negotiate your deal. If they don't, I would question their motives. When you actually close the deal, you will have an "in" with that agent, who may consider representing you in the future.

Inside View

"I got my first job, then I got an agent. A friend of mine who was working recommended me to an agent. They negotiated the deal and became my agent. If you know anybody with any reasonable degree of success, they can recommend someone."

—MARK MILLER

PITCHING

If you have done the work, acquired an agent, and piqued the interest of an industry insider, you may be invited to a pitch meeting. I suggest you review the section in the previous chapter on pitching for television. Many of the same rules apply, except that in a film, unlike in a television episode, nothing is established—not the characters, their relationships, or situations. A film pitch, then, has to establish all of these elements. That's why it's good to have a short version, a medium version, and a long version of your ideas. If the person you're pitching to seems intrigued, expand on your idea. If not, move on to the next idea.

Listen to criticism—try to work with it and to hear the critics' point of view. You don't have to agree with the criticism, but the information might help you in future pitch meetings with them or with other producers. Even if you don't make a sale, you may get a recommendation that improves your writing or a referral that expands your network of contacts. Filmmaking is a collaborative effort. A pitch meeting is a good starting point for learning what cooperation entails.

I do suggest that you know who you're pitching to. Whether you have been referred by an agent or sent through a contact, it's important to know what the company produces and whether it is a legitimate operation. If you share your ideas with people who aren't real players or mail ideas to unknown entities, you may be giving your work away.

INSIDE VIEW

"Look out for places that just want you to pitch ideas. If you're sending your work to a listing service or blindly in the mail, you're basically *giving* someone a couple of hundred dollars. Ideas can't be copyrighted, and they can be picked up and worked on by someone else."

—AUDREY KELLY

OUTLINES AND TREATMENTS

If a producer or production company express interest in your work after a pitch meeting, the production company will pay you to develop an outline or a treatment. This is the beginning of a deal, so, if possible, have your agent negotiate for you. You might want to practice writing an outline and treatment as part of your overall scriptwriting practice.

An outline documents the beginning, middle, and end of the story. It reviews the major scenes and action in chronological order. The treatment is a detailed plot description that grows from the outline. It is written like a short story and should reflect your writing style and ability.

It's a good idea to practice these formats, especially if you have more ideas than time to write. An idea that you develop in outline or treatment form could be valuable to a production company sometime in the future.

RESOURCES

Trade Magazines and Directories

Hollywood Creative Directory. 3000 Olympic Blvd., Santa Monica CA 90404. Tel: 310-315-4815. This company produces several directories that list production companies, representation possibilities, and other resources.

Daily Variety and *Weekly Variety*. 5700 Wilshire Blvd., Suite 120, Los Angeles CA 90036. Tel: 213-857-6600. Industry news in all fields of entertainment. *Daily Variety* features an updated list of production companies and their current and upcoming projects.

The Hollywood Reporter. 5505 Wilshire Blvd., Los Angeles CA 90036. Tel: 213-525-2000. Insider industry news and a listing of production companies.

Ross Reports Television. Television Index, Inc., 40-29 27th St., Long Island City NY 11101. Tel: 718-937-3990. Although this monthly report focuses on television, it also includes an updated listing of agents.

Scenario, The Magazine of Screenwriting Art. 3200 Tower Oaks Blvd., Rockville MD 20852-9789. Tel: 800-222-2654. Each issue of this monthly magazine features interviews with writers, a keynote essay from a prominent film personality, and four complete screenplays.

Premiere. Premiere Subscription Dept., P.O. Box 55389, Boulder CO 80323-5389. An entertaining magazine devoted to all aspects of filmmaking.

The New York Screenwriter Publications. 545 8th Avenue, Suite 401, New York NY 10018. Tel: 800-418-5637. Articles about writing and the film business are featured in this company's savvy magazine, which also offers information on conferences, legal resources and writing contests.

Books

Writer's Market. F&W Publications, 1507 Dana Avenue, Cincinnati OH 45207. This resource for writers offers a special section on submission options for scriptwriters.

Grammar of Film Language by Daniel Arijon. $22.95. Silman-James Press, distributed by Samuel French, Inc., 7623 Sunset Blvd., Hollywood CA 90046. A guide to the visual techniques of directing, editing, and cinematography. Good for writers who want to learn how stories can be told visually.

How to Make It in Hollywood—Everything you need to know about agents, managers, lawyers, chutzpa, schmoozing, the casting couch, the Godfather call, rhino skin, handling rejection, how to be lucky and all the steps you need to achieve the success you deserve by Linda Buzzell. $11.00. A Harper Perennial, a division of HarperCollins Publishers, 10 E. 53rd St., New York NY 10022.

Lew Hunter's Screenwriting 434 by Lew Hunter. $13.95. A Perigee Book. The Berkley Publishing Group, 200 Madison Avenue, New York NY 10016. This book was recommended by *everyone* in the film industry.

Screenplay: The Foundations of Screenwriting—A Step-by-Step Guide from Concept to Finished Scripts by Syd Field. $11.95. A Dell trade paperback. Bantam Doubleday Dell Publishing Group, 1540 Broadway, New York NY 10036.

Selling a Screenplay: The Screenwriter's Guide to Hollywood—How to Pitch, Sell and Market Your Screenplay by Syd Field. $11.95. A Dell trade paperback. Bantam Doubleday Dell Publishing Group, 1540 Broadway, New York NY 10036.

The Screenwriter's Workbook by Syd Field. $10.95. A Dell trade paperback. Bantam Doubleday Dell Publishing Group, 1540 Broadway, New York NY 10036. Exercises and step-by-step instruction for creating a successful screenplay.

Making a Good Script Great by Linda Seger. $12.95. Samuel French Inc., 7623 Sunset Blvd., Hollywood CA 90046. A guide to writing and rewriting by a Hollywood script consultant.

From Script to Screen: The Collaborative Art of Filmmaking by Linda Seger and Edward Jay Whetmore. $14.95. An Owl book. Henry Holt & Company, 115 W. 18th St., New York NY 10011.

Writing Screenplays That Sell by Michael Hauge. $13.00. A Harper Perennial. HarperCollins Publishers, 10 E. 53rd St., New York NY 10022.

Adventures in the Screen Trade: A Personal View of Hollywood and Screenwriting by William Goldman. $15.99. Warner Books, P.O. Box 690, New York NY 10019. A personal favorite by the "nobody knows nothing" king of screenwriting.

The Hollywood Reporter Yearly Blue Book. $59.95 plus $4.95 for shipping. Blue Book Orders, Circulation Dept., 5055 Wilshire Blvd., Los Angeles CA 90036. Tel: 213-525-2150. A film, TV, and video directory.

The Elements of Screenwriting: A guide for film and television writing by Irwin R. Blacker. $5.95. Collier Books, Macmillan Publishing Co., 866 3rd Avenue, New York NY 10022.

Hollywood Creative Directory Guide to Producers, Studios, Network Executives, and Production Companies. $45.00. Hollywood Creative Directory, 3000 Olympic Blvd., Suite 2525, Santa Monica CA 90404. Tel: 310-315-4815.

Organizations

The Writers Guild of America. East Tel: 212-767-7800; West Tel: 310-550-1000. This organization offers registration services to protect your work. For members, it supplies industry practice and payment standards for contracts and negotiations, writing fellowships, symposiums, panel discussions, and awards programs. Call for details and membership criteria. The Writers Guild East covers writers who live east of the Mississippi. Writers living west of the Mississippi are covered by the Writers Guild West.

The Writers Network. 289 South Robertson Blvd., Suite 465, Beverly Hills CA 90211. Tel: 310-275-0287. A growing organization created by writers. Features a newsletter, seminars, and services to help writers improve their work and find producers. This is an extremely helpful organization, especially for new writers.

Catalogs
Script City. Tel: 800-676-2522. Offers thousands of movie and television scripts, as well as books, seminars on tape, and writer's software.

Book City. Tel: 800-4-CINEMA. Carries a large selection of screenplays and movie books.

The Drama Bookshop. 723 7th Avenue, New York NY 10019. Tel: 212-944-0595 or 800-322-0595. Offers a large selection of all forms of entertainment-oriented books.

Chapter 4

On Stage:

Learning the Art of Playwriting

AUTHOR, AUTHOR!

STEPHANIE KLAPPER
Director, Manhattan Punch Line One Act Comedy Festival, Alice's Fourth Floor, UBU Rep., Double Image One Act Festival, Theater of the Open Eye, and Ensemble Studio Theater
Casting Director, Long Wharf Theater, The Old Globe in San Diego, WPA Theater, Jewish Repertory, and numerous Broadway, off-Broadway, film, and television shows

MARY HARDEN
Literary Agent, Brett Adams Limited; clients include: Robert Harling (*Steel Magnolias*), Eugene Lee (*Texas Hot Links*), Barbara Lebow (*A Shayna Madel*), and Mary Gallagher (TV movie *Nobody's Child*)

MARK RIHERD
Institute Director, Ensemble Studio Theater Institute for Professional Training
Arts Administration Consultant, Studio in a School and INTAR, The Hispanic-American Art Center

JAMES RYAN
Playwright: *Dennis, Arab Bride, Portrait of My Bikini, Iron Tommy, Door Cuba, Celestial Navigation;* his work has been produced at Circle Repertory Theater, Ensemble Studio Theater, Berkeley Stage, Playwrights Horizon, Playwrights Center in Minneapolis, and Stage Three.
Teacher, EST, The 42nd Street Collection, Lincoln Theater Institute

CAROL TURTURRO
Playwright: *This End Up, One Sings Opera The Other Plays Deaf, Goodbye Honey,* and *Life in Still Pots*; her work has been produced at Playwrights Horizon, The Harold Curlman Theater, EST, The Women in America Project.

• • •

Could you imagine the American theater without Neil Simon? Even if you aren't a fan, you have to acknowledge the importance of his contributions to playwriting. He is a symbol of the importance of the playwright with a comic voice to the life blood of theater. A comedy can tackle any subject and sometimes does it more effectively than a drama because humor conveys a dramatic message more easily. The comic play can be both frivolous and moving. In the arena of live theater, a comedy can be powerful because the audience can't be passive. The action is too close, too intimate.

I begin with these thoughts because I feel that the comedic voice in theater is often overlooked by the beginning writer. If you love theater and truly have your own voice, you should explore it. Think of these recent comedic plays as inspiration:

Jeffrey: Portrays relationships in the age of AIDS.
The Sisters Rosenzweig: Explores the complex network of family dynamics.
Marvin's Room: Deals with loss, death, and the notion of living for others.

All of these plays have belly laughs and bite. Now consider:

All in the Timing: Combines word play and intellectualism that questions beliefs and culture.
I Hate Hamlet: A tremendous "What if . . ." that comments on personal values.

Mastergate: Satirizes and parodies our political system.
Lend Me a Tenor: A farce set in the world of opera.

I have chosen these examples because they reflect the diversity of comedy in theater. The scripts are readily available.

THE MARKET

The high cost of production has led to a massive change in the business of theater. Broadway is producing fewer plays than ever before. Productions that have successful runs on the Great White Way usually originate in small repertory companies or regional theaters. This is good news for the playwright working outside New York, who may be able to get his work produced in regional theaters such as Steppenwolf in Chicago or the La Jolla Playhouse in San Diego. Playwrights no longer need to be based in New York to succeed. If you are an aspiring playwright, you must focus on improving your writing and embracing the theatrical community nearest you.

HOW TO START: EMBRACING THE THEATRICAL COMMUNITY

Theater is a collaborative art, and exposure to its inner workings is crucial for the writer who needs to understand how a play develops and is finally realized. It's tough when you start in the theater as a writer, particularly since you probably haven't yet written a piece worthy of being produced. You should get involved in the theater world in any way possible—whether it's being an usher or carrying props. You can also get involved by taking classes at a theater school, volunteering at a theater company or community theater, or starting a theater group on your own. Actually, starting your own theater group isn't that difficult. You can recruit actors and production people from schools and arts organizations. Certainly, you shouldn't try full-fledged productions in the beginning. But even if the group meets periodically to read famous works aloud, it's a worthwhile experience since you'll be connecting with people who love the theater. Over time you can work toward producing a play that involves the members of your group as actors, designers, and writers.

INSIDE VIEW

"I think it's important to get to know as many people as you can. One good way is to volunteer to be a reader* at a theater company or in any aspect. Getting to know people will get your work read more seriously. Everything I've accomplished has come from my involvement in the theater community."

—CAROL TURTURRO

(*A reader reviews submissions and writes reports on the plays that have production potential.)

Involvement in any form of the theatrical community will provide you with an outlet to improve your work and grow as a writer. It will also expose you to what working in a theater is really like. The experience will allow you to evaluate whether this is the area you wish to focus on. In addition, you will begin the important process of networking.

INVOKE YOUR FAVORITE WRITER'S AFFIRMATION: WRITE, WRITE, WRITE TO PERFECT YOUR CRAFT

In the beginning it will be difficult to write on a daily basis. As a playwright you need to develop technically through training, emotionally through life experience, and artistically through honing your ability to tell a story creatively. This takes time, but if you are a writer, you should be in the habit of writing. As you progress, you will find that your work takes shape. Will it be a great play? That can only be determined by the depth of your talent and the time you invest in writing.

PERPETUAL STUDYING

Good writers are perpetual students in school and life experience. Attending theater schools or working in a theatrical company will teach you about theater as a business, the history of theater, the importance of collaboration, and how to define your playwriting voice.

The lessons of life experience are also valid training tools. The more emotions and experiences you have, the more material you will have to draw on for your work. As you read newspapers and books and see movies and plays, you will experience millions of situations that, with your creative twist, can be transformed into great plays. This was successfully done by John Gauré in *Six Degrees of Separation*. You have to study people, the problems they encounter, their character traits, and the way they speak. If you want your work to ring true, it has to grow from reality, even if, in the end, you abstract it to an extreme. The audience will relate to the reality that you depict.

INSIDE VIEW

"You want to read constantly, both contemporary and classic plays. A lot of skill work is reinforced that way. This will help you find the genre you are interested in. Also, read the biographies of playwrights to understand their thoughts. See as much theater as you can. You actually learn more from a bad play. Finally, you have to grow as a person because as a playwright you have to draw from your experience."

—MARK RIHERD

EDUCATION AND TRAINING

As discussed, all of life is a playwright's school, and therefore any class in sociology, psychology, or anthropology can enlighten you about people, their motivations and their lives. Keep in mind that all forms of writing instruction are helpful to the beginner playwright. For example, learning how to draft a short story or novel is a valuable way to polish your storytelling skills. You will discover that while you still need to learn the specifics of playwriting, the experiences you have in different forms of writing will give you a heightened sense of working within the medium.

As far as structured school programs are concerned, the Yale School of Drama is a great choice, but tuition is expensive and it requires a two-year commitment. There are other options—taking classes at a local college, attending workshops, and so forth. When deciding whether or not to attend a class or school, evaluate the following criteria:

- The class emphasizes the use of structure, dialogue, character, and plot in an integrated manner.
- The instructors are working in theater, and they have something to offer both as teachers and as writers.
- The teachers and students create an atmosphere that is conducive to writing.
- The teachers suggest how to improve your work to bring out *your* voice—not echo others' or impose theirs.

- The school offers classes in acting, directing, and design. You should take these classes to understand how your writing will interact with other aspects of theatrical production.
- The class offers a sense of theater and playwriting history. You can learn a tremendous amount through studying the classics.
- Teachers and students provide feedback as often as possible. This is the best way to assess if you're conveying your intended message and whether your work affects others.
- The program offers outlets for your work to be produced, even if it's a staged reading in class to an invited audience.
- The instructors understand the luxury of failure. You must be allowed to learn from your mistakes. The learning process involves understanding the specific reasons why something doesn't work.

If all of these factors are in place, a school program will give you an accurate taste of what it is like to work in the theater. In addition to any classroom training, reading and attending plays are vital to your development as a writer. Don't limit yourself to comedies. Learning about structure, dialogue, and plot development in dramas will reinforce what's needed for a successful comedic play.

Keep in mind that feedback is also available outside the classroom situation. Invite your friends to a staged reading in your living room. When you solicit feedback from friends, remember that they are offering a gut reaction, not an intellectual debate. A writers' group may also be helpful in this regard. Of course you should ignore any feedback that is scathing, overly critical, or offered by people who seek to impose their beliefs on you.

INSIDE VIEW

"Find one good teacher anyplace you can—someone who is interested in offering you strategies for you to give your work pulse. This attitude should be 'How can we take your voice and bring it to life?' They should make you excited about going home and working. If not, move on."

—JAMES RYAN

CONFERENCES, WORKSHOPS, AND SEMINARS

Conferences, workshops, and seminars expose you to varying points of view and offer you the opportunity to network with other attendees. As you consider attending these events you have to assess cost and your learning priorities. Here are some guidelines:

1. Are the speakers or teachers working in the theater world?

2. What is the quality of the material that will be presented? If it's a company or writer whose work you don't value, the program would be a waste of your time.
3. Will there be a chance to meet and network with other professionals?
4. Is the conference, workshop, or seminar well organized? Does the brochure outline information in such a way that you can tell that the information offered and the overall mission of the event would be beneficial to your writing?

Only when you weigh these factors can you make the right decision. If you are involved in the theater community and reading trade magazines, you will have no trouble finding out about upcoming events.

WRITERS' GROUPS

A writers' group is an excellent forum for getting feedback and learning structure. Playwriting can't be done in a vacuum. A successful play must engage an audience. If you join or even start a group, set up feedback rules and allot reading time. It is important to remember that feedback should focus on whether the writer's dialogue, characters, motivation, and plot are sharp and in keeping with what the playwright is trying to convey. A group situation should not be used for personal attacks or for forcing beliefs upon others.

THE PLAY'S THE THING

How do you write a great play? Obviously there is no formula, or it would happen more often. It's all a reflection of the playwright's creative process. Initially this will be unclear, but as you continue to expose yourself to the theater and life's experiences, and combine that with your unwavering commitment to your writing, your creative process will emerge. Will you produce a classic? It's not guaranteed. But if you work hard, you will write the best play you can. That's why theater, like every art form, has to be a passion. Success can be elusive, but fulfilling your need to write a play is an attainable goal.

AGENTS

Since theatrical productions involve great expense and lots of different, creative people, getting your work produced is a very complicated process. An agent plays the vital role of connecting you to producers and theater companies and making sure all the pieces fit together. In the beginning, you should not seek representation. First you need material. This does not necessarily mean your first draft of a play. By material I mean a finished piece that is strong enough to reflect potential for production.

If you can identify the agent you want to work with and you have worthwhile material in your repertoire, you should send a query letter about your work. Your chances of making a great impression on the agent will improve if your letter coincides with something happening in your professional life that validates your prospective project. An invitation to a reading or, if applicable, a mention that you are under consideration for an award or grant are good examples of factors that will pique an agent's interest.

You might be surprised to know that agents will approach you. If your work is being read or performed by your theater school or small companies, it may be seen by an agent or agency scout. If an agent approaches you, don't make a hasty decision. Find out about the agent through your network of contacts in the theater community. An agent is only as useful as his or her ability to get your work read by producers. You will also have to assess the agent's reputation and whether you could work well together.

If you're at the point of having your play produced, contracts suddenly become a part of your life. Don't assume that your agent always has your best interests in mind. Review any contracts or legal issues with an entertainment lawyer or with one of the writing organizations listed in the Resources section at the end of this chapter.

SUBMITTING

If securing representation proves difficult, you may want to submit your work directly. Being active in the theater community ensures that you are connecting with people who can get you information about theater festivals, contests, and small companies looking for new plays. Also, if you follow the trade theater publications you will find a number of outlets for submitting your work.

INSIDE VIEW

"The first step is a letter of inquiry. I don't care if it's clever. It should give a good synopsis of the piece, a recommendation from someone in the business, and an indication that something significant is happening in the writer's career. This could be a reading, a production, press about the writer, or an award. This indicates that the person has worked and is ready. A bad thing is when I get a letter or phone call that says I have three sketches. I prefer getting plays so I can see if the writer has a voice and can develop characters. If I do work with someone, I believe in numbers. I try to get the script to as many people as possible. I don't want to prejudice it looking for just one, two, or three people who will love it."

—MARY HARDEN

If an organization's submission guidelines are unclear, call to find out specifics such as what type of plays they accept and the suggested length. Some organizations are looking for plays that have a particular point of view. There's no point in sending a one-act comedy about a major league baseball team to a company looking for dramas about women's issues. Yes, they may like your writing, but if they are submission-heavy, they probably will not read it.

In the beginning, a simple query explaining your play and how it fits that company's, festival's, or contest's guidelines is the best introduction. Submit a script only if asked or instructed to. Send a self-addressed stamped envelope to make sure your material is returned, and, to protect yourself, copyright your play at the Writers Guild East or West.

THE PRODUCTION

The truly wonderful aspect of the theater is that it remains the writer's medium. Unlike film, where the writer may be called back if needed later on in the production process, the playwright plays an active role in the collaboration. Now the key here is *collaboration,* because first and foremost, a play is a group effort. The idea the playwright has about how a line should be delivered may not make sense when the line is spoken by an actor on a stage. The difference between page and performance can be vast. As a play is brought to life, a playwright must make changes. Actors, directors, and stage design people will contribute their expertise, which in most cases is not within the writer's realm of experience. A successful writer should not allow his ego to get in the way. Fine-tuning and adjusting is an enormously important part of the production process.

There is, of course, room for disagreement. The director, actors, or producer may ask you to make changes you feel are unnecessary. If this should occur, don't act too quickly. Let these suggestions sink in for a while to see if they might really make sense. Give yourself an opportunity to visualize making the changes. Consult experts in your circle of theater contacts whose opinions you value.

If you are positive the suggested change is wrong, you have to decide how strongly you want to hold your ground. You may want to have your agent intervene and make your intentions or thoughts clear. Resist the urge to have a temper tantrum. Ask yourself if you feel strongly enough about the proposed change to stop or slow down a production. Generally, when this occurs, a compromise is reached. Sometimes writers have to make changes in a play only to see that the original draft was indeed better. It's all part of the discovery process.

This is a difficult scenario for the newcomer who has never participated in a collaboration. Even if you've never had your work produced, being involved in the theater community and keeping an eye on the business should offer you insight into the production process. In preliminary meetings, make sure your interpretations are in sync with those of the producers, directors, and actors. Don't agree to have your work used for a production that will be done in a style you are not happy with and think all will work out when you finally express your opinion. If you have some knowledge of how to cultivate the shared theatrical vision, you will find the production process much more satisfying.

INSIDE VIEW

"As both a director and casting director working with new writers, I find it's often difficult for playwrights to give up their laugh lines. This can be problematic, but when rehearsing the play, material that doesn't fit becomes obvious. It is important for the author to have a collaborative relationship with the director in terms of reaching the goal of an enjoyable, successful production on all levels. In the ideal situation, the playwright's vision is enhanced by the director, actors, and designers. This is why it's crucial for the playwright and director to be in communication with each other before rehearsal. This way the development period will proceed smoothly. It's important for playwrights to know that the people they're working with have the same vision and sense of comedy. It's unfortunate to watch a gifted comic author's work interpreted in a dark, somber, unfunny way."

—STEPHANIE KLAPPER

RESOURCES

Books

The Playwright's Art: Conversations With Contemporary Dramatists edited by Jackson R. Bryer. $16.95. Rutgers University Press, 109 Church St., New Brunswick NJ 08901. In-depth interviews with A.R. Gurney, Wendy Wasserstein, Terrance McNally, Beth Henley, John Guare, Neil Simon, and others.

Writing Your First Play by Roger A. Hall. $22.95. Focal Press, Butterworth-Heineman, 80 Montvale Avenue, Stoneham MA 02180. A professor of theater at James Madison University provides a step-by-step guide to writing your first play.

The Art of Dramatic Writing by Lajos Egri. $10.95. Simon & Schuster, 1230 Avenue of the Americas, New York NY 10020. Recommended by all the theater insiders interviewed for this section, this guide offers a unique and inspiring insight into the craft of playwriting.

Poetics by Aristotle, translated with an introduction by Gerald F. Else. $10.95. An Ann Arbor paperback. University of Michigan Press, 839 Greene St., Ann Arbor MI 48106. This is a staple for most playwriting classes and one you should consult for timeless advice.

Meisner on Acting by Sanford Meisner. $11.00. Random House, 201 E. 50th St., New York NY 10022. Any insight into acting is a great help to playwrights. Sanford

Meisner's technique is a good starting point for understanding the basics of acting.

Magazines
Theater Week. 28 W. 25th St., 4th Floor, New York NY 10010. A colorful periodical covering all the aspects of the world of theater. It provides insight into actors, writers, directors, and the production process.

American Theater. 355 Lexington Avenue, New York NY 10017. Offers an expansive view of stagecraft, productions, and the industry.

Catalogs
The Drama Bookshop, 723 7th Avenue, New York NY 10019. Tel: 212-944-0595 or 800-322-0595. This shop and mail order service offers a huge selection of books on all topics relating to theater.

Samuel French, Inc. 7623 West Sunset Blvd., Hollywood CA 90046. Tel: 213-876-0570. This publisher and book mail-order service provides titles dealing with all areas of theater, writing, production, and stagecraft.

Organizations
The Dramatists Guild. 234 W. 44th St., New York NY 10036-3909. Tel: 212-398-9366. Offers business and legal advice, and information on marketing, royalty collection, and symposiums with theater professionals. The Guild publishes newsletters and resource directories.

New Dramatists. 424 W. 44th St., New York NY 10036. Tel: 212-757-6960. Programs and services include readings, workshops, fellowships, and library resources. Grants and awards are offered to talented new playwrights.

Directories

Handel's National Directory for the Performing Arts. $250.00. R. R. Bowker, Reed Reference Publishing, 121 Chanlon Road, New Providence NJ 07974. This extensive resource directory provides information on theater organizations and educational institutions around the country. It may be available in drama schools, performing arts libraries, or in the general reference section of your local library.

Association of Authors' Representatives. 10 Astor Place, 3rd Floor, New York NY 10003. Tel: 212-353-3709. The A.A.R. has a membership list of agents who follow a mutual cannon of ethics for working with writers. Call for a copy of the membership list or for their helpful brochures "The Role of the Literary Agent" and "How to Get an Agent."

Literary Agents: A Writer's Guide by Adam Begley. $12.99. A Penguin book. Penguin USA, 375 Hudson St., New York NY 10014.

Ross Reports Television. Television Index, Inc., 40-29 27th St., Long Island City NY 11101. Tel: 718-937-3990. Although this monthly report focuses on television, it also includes updated listings of agents.

Chapter 5

By the Book:

Humor Books and Novels

THE EDITORIAL BOARD

JANE CAVELINA
Senior Editor, Crown Publishers
Author: *Growing Up Catholic, More Growing Up Catholic, Still Catholic After All These Years, How to Really Watch The Godfather*

JENNIFER ENDERLIN
Senior Editor, St. Martin's Press

DAN GOODMAN
Author: *Meditations for Miserable People Who Want to Stay That Way, Meditations for a Miserable Millennium*

PAUL ROSA
Author: *Idiot Letters: One Man's Relentless Assault on Corporate America*

BRUCE TRACY
Senior Editor, Doubleday Books

BARBARA-J ZITWER
Literary Agent, The Barbara-J Zitwer Agency

•   •   •

If you really want to impress people, tell them you're publishing a book. It was probably the high point of my life. Suddenly everyone thought I was literate, intelligent, and soon to be rich. Never mind that it was a small humor book. This mystique is especially great for your family, friends and even the public, but writers should view the world of book publishing for what it is: a business motivated by profit incentives. If you want to publish a book, prepare by working on your writing and learning as much you can about the business.

THE MARKET

For the comedy writer, the obvious choice is humor books. Small in size—comedy loves brevity—these books are often located in the the humor section of the bookstore or close to the cash register in point-of-purchase displays. The former is not the ideal spot, since your humor book could get lost in a sea of satirical titles. The major players in this genre are writers whose followings have developed through their syndicated newspaper columns. Dave Barry, Erma Bombeck, and the late Lewis Grizzard have carved out sizable niches in this area. For the beginning writer, there is only one way to separate yourself from the pack—come up with a great idea.

This great idea or "high concept" must be fully understood in one sentence. The book buyer has to be able to read the title and relate to the idea immediately. *Politically Incorrect Bedtime Stories, French for Cats,* and *The*

Southern Belle Primer are the best examples of books conceived by clever writers with offbeat, high-concept ideas.

Often, humor books satirize established books, films, television shows, or cultural icons. Some examples include:

Everything I Ever Wanted to Know I Learned on Star Trek, a funny take on the best-selling book *All I Really Need to Know I Learned in Kindergarten* and the television show *Star Trek; Life's Little Destruction Book,* inspired by *Life's Little Instruction Book;* and *Omnibus,* a parody of the film *Forrest Gump.* All is fair game in satire. Self-help books, advice books, even business books are likely targets for clever writers. *The Seven Habits of Highly Effective People,* for instance, was reborn as *The Seven Habits of Highly Defective People.*

Finally, there are the joke books. *The Bathroom Reader, Snaps,* and *Truly Tasteless Jokes* are just a few memorable titles. All of these books, which consist of jokes strung together under an umbrella theme, have sold so successfully they have spawned sequels.

Humor books also can be made up of short items—essays, lists, recipes, letters, ads, and so forth. Readers need only pick up the book, turn to any page, and laugh. Catchy cover design and a reasonable price—usually $7.00 for a small-sized paperback—make these books even more appealing.

Although books by Bill Cosby, Jerry Seinfeld, and Paul Reiser have had a strong presence on best-seller lists, new writers should be wary about following in their footsteps. These authors are established television stars, and each has a built-in audience interested in his point of view. Their readers are buying a known quantity and won't be deterred by long formats.

INSIDE VIEW

"Packaging plays an important role in comic writing. Fiction and humor books are very different. In humor books, high concept is everything. The attention span for the consumer is seconds. They flip it open, glance, and if it doesn't appeal, they don't buy it. The design, the humor, and the idea have to all accomplish this."

—BRUCE TRACY

The comedic novel is yet another forum for comedy writing, but creating a comic voice in fiction differs greatly from short-form humor writing. A series of jokes strung together is not enough to sustain a reader's interest throughout a novel-length story. In a novel, the humor must evolve from the characters, their motivations, and the situations they find themselves in. This is most clearly demonstrated in classics such as *Confederacy of Dunces* or *Catch-22*. While these books may cause you to laugh out loud, they fully flesh out the characters and plot in specific ways. The humor is organic and comes directly from the action or characters' points of view. Writing comedic fiction is not about incorporating a series of funny lines into the text. A really gifted writer knows how to fully integrate humor into the story in a natural, subtle way.

INSIDE VIEW

"You can argue that Ann Tyler's novels are humorous because of the quirky characters and situations, but in the humorous novel there are ranges. They can also be farcical as with *Tom Jones* and *Joseph Andrews*. The writer is trying to find a narrative that's believable for an entire novel. The comic structure is all about constraints. This works best when the humor comes from the character."

—BRUCE TRACY

The fiction market is highly competitive. Thousands of novels are published each year, and only a handful of titles become best-sellers. What contributes to the making of a best-seller? Certainly, an established fiction writer with a loyal following has an advantage. First novels rarely find their way onto the best-seller list. Occasionally a publisher will back a first novel with an aggressive publicity and marketing campaign. This doesn't guarantee a best-seller, but frequently the strategy works.

HOW TO START

The Humor Book

The first step in writing a short-form humor book is to familiarize yourself with the marketplace. This means spending a great deal of time in the humor section of the bookstore to get a strong sense of the genre. Doing some field work will also save you from working on an idea that has already been done. Now that I'm a bit more established and have relationships with several editors, I often run ideas by them. I'm frequently surprised by how many of my ideas already have been used. But you have to take it to the next level. It's not just the idea, it's how it's done. Your point of view and your comic voice are the most important aspects of a humor book. A great little idea that's poorly executed might become a book, but it won't reach the widest audience. Your mission as a writer is to find an idea and a voice that readers can relate to.

INSIDE VIEW

"I'm always trying to come up with new ideas. The humor market is wide, and you want to appeal to the mainstream. So you pull back on the edgy humor; anything that is off-color and offensive could make an editor uncomfortable."

—DAN GOODMAN

Where do ideas come from? Look at the world around you and satirize, exaggerate, and imitate while writing in your own distinctive style. The trick is to create humor that's funny, not just to you but to others.

Humor is always a numbers game. I always overwrite humor—not each piece, but the number of pieces. Comedy is very subjective, and in the end you want to create the material with the most appeal. By rewriting and refining it, the material will develop in many different ways. The actual writing process will also help you assess if your idea has legs—if it really has book-length potential, which in general is about 100 pages.

INSIDE VIEW

"Humor writing is all your point of view. Funny makes you laugh. You can't fake it. Think about the things that make you laugh, something close in your life that comes from your heart that others will think is funny too. Then research it. Magazine articles, even serious ones, will give you all the aspects of a topic. You need a lot of raw material. Pour in all the information and let it synthesize."

—JANE CAVELINA

Start by coming up with a subject and research your topic in the library, gathering all the information you can find. Write a funny take on each aspect of your subject. For example, if the theme of your book is dating, then blind dates, the dating game, senior dating, and dating octogenarians are just a few of the avenues you can explore. The more information you have, the more you can invent comic possibilities. Organize the various categories of your umbrella theme into outline form and go to work. As you develop your ideas and conceive new ones, you may have to alter your original theme. Go with it.

The Novel

How do you write the great American novel? Although many try, few finish. It's no easy feat. As with most long-form writing, reading the classics is the best way to begin. Although humor is your focus, the books you read for inspiration don't have to be funny. What you're really exploring is storytelling, characters, plot, and style. Your comic voice will be a natural by-product of your writing style.

Decide how you plan to structure your novel. It can be written in a traditional narrative form, or as a series of letters, diary entries, or even reports. The structure of a novel propels the story. Tone is another factor that requires careful consideration. Is your book going to be an outlandish farce or a subtle comedy? Will you create characters who are overtly humorous, or are the characters rendered funny by the dire or ridiculous situations they find themselves in? Conceptualizing how you want to tell a story before you even come up with a plot idea seems tricky, but it's a logical way to formulate your ideas. Over the years I've heard a great many rules of writing. Here are the top three:

- Write about a scenario you know.
- Write from experience.
- Write every day.

These are valid general guidelines. But do they make sense for you? Personally, I'm creative in a more abstract way. I like to think that if I feed my mind as much as possible, my imagination will crystallize the story I want to tell. I do believe in writing every day. Whatever stage you're at, you should be spending a great deal of time writing. The combination of writing and reading and analyzing the form and content of great works of fiction will polish your writing skills.

When you conceive of an idea and decide on a format, map out your story in outline form. Flesh out the characters and plot sequences. When the beginning, middle, and end of your story are clearly outlined, work to embellish your outline into scenes or events. Then begin writing chapters. You'll figure out fairly quickly whether your ideas and outline are substantial enough to merit full-length treatment.

For some, this step-by-step approach to novel writing is too pragmatic. I spoke to one writer who said his writing is an outgrowth of random chapter ideas. Any method is valid, as long as it works for you. When I write, I need an outline that helps me resolve which way I'm headed. I realize, however, the importance of remaining flexible. An ending can change, and scenes, characters, and events can grow in different directions. That's okay. Set up guideposts, but don't be afraid to alter your course. Let your talent and intuition guide you.

INSIDE VIEW

"The humor novelist has a unique take on the world. It shows up on every page. The plot has to work on its own. The jokes have to emerge from the plot, characters, and situations. It can't be a commentary, but it must reflect the human condition."

—JANE CAVELINA

EDUCATION AND TRAINING

Publishing is a competitive market, and any classroom work that helps you hone your writing skills and stand out from the crowd is valuable. For the short-form humor book writer, improvisation and stand-up classes and sitcom workshops teach useful skills.

If you're interested in writing fiction, look for writing classes and programs that can help you develop your voice as a storyteller. The ideal class should teach the classics—structure, character, and plot—but the emphasis should be on the development of your own distinctive style. Writing novels is a creative pursuit, and a school that churns out students in cookie-cutter fashion won't help you get ahead. Go where your unique voice will be nurtured.

Before enrolling in a class or program for either long- or short-form writing, be sure to ask the following questions to ensure you are receiving the best education possible:

- Are the instructors published writers?
- Does the class curriculum reflect what you need to learn?
- Is the cost worth what is being offered?
- Will there be opportunities to meet and learn from editors or other publishing professionals to gain insight into the business?
- Does the class help you prepare for submitting material to agents and editors?
- Have any writers whose work and judgment you respect attended the classes?

Keep in mind that these are guidelines. For the real inside scoop, speak to students who have studied at these schools to get a sense of what they have learned.

THE PROPOSAL

In order for a book to be sold, it must be pitched to an agent or editor. But before you can pitch a book, you must submit a proposal. This can be of any length, depending on how much is needed to assure the agent or editor you know your subject, write well, and have a sense of how the project will take form. In the last year, I have sold three books on proposals (this is easier for nonfiction writers like myself than for the novelist). One proposal was twenty-four pages long, the second two pages long, and the third just two sentences. The proposal must contain enough information for the project to be visualized in its entirety.

INSIDE VIEW

"We read humor book proposals out loud in editorial meetings to see if something makes the group laugh. It would be beneficial for writers to work in the same way. Get a group to read the material. Also, see what's selling in a phenomenal way and look at it in a twisted sense to see how you can make fun of it. It's great when someone can satirize a trend the audience can relate to and laugh at. *Life's Little Destruction Book* is a great example."

—JENNIFER ENDERLIN

The Humor Book

Your proposal should begin with a short description of your book idea so the publisher can get a sense of your subject and comedic angle. One or two sentences should suffice. Then create an outline or chapter breakdown of the book. Next, I think it's effective to include a few sample pages from each chapter, but you may opt to complete a few chapters in their entirety. In addition to presenting your comedic idea with clarity, your proposal must accomplish one other thing—it has to make the editor laugh!

The Novel

The novel proposal is a very different story. It is extremely difficult for an unknown writer to sell a novel on a proposal, or "partial," as it's called in the business. It does happen, but the fact is, editors have to know you can write the entire book. This is tough to do, but just showing a few chapters may not be reassuring enough to the editor. In addition, how can you convince someone else you can write a novel if you haven't yet proven it to yourself? Learn your craft, write your novel, and don't worry about selling it until after it's finished.

SUBMITTING

When you complete your proposal or your novel, you'll ask yourself the dreaded question—how do I get it published? As you study the market by reading magazines such as *Publishers Weekly, Writer's Digest, The Writer,* and *The New York Times Book Review,* you should make lists of agents and publishers you want to work with. You can also consider contacting agents, publishers, or even other writers through the networking you've done at conferences, schools, and writing groups. Keep in mind my theory of six degrees of separation. Who do you know who can get your proposal or novel into the hands of the right agent or publisher?

INSIDE VIEW

"To find an agent I went to the library and looked at a book that listed agencies and contacts. I sent a letter to The Agency for Performing Arts, ICM, and William Morris. Two of them never got back to me. Lisa Bankoff at ICM called me three or four days later and asked me for more material. Two weeks later she said she would shop it around. She did, and it came down to three editors bidding for it."

—PAUL ROSA

I would suggest first trying to get an agent. This might seem like an impossible feat, but if you think your book is good enough to be published, so should an agent. You can look up listings of agents in the *Literary Market Place* and other resources listed at the end of this chapter. Before sending your proposal or novel to an agency, call to find out the submission procedure. Some agents do not accept unsolicited material. Others only consider new clients who come to them through personal recommendations. Go through your networking list and see if you can find someone who is acquainted with a literary agent. Believe me, some of the biggest agencies will read your work if you present it well and demonstrate that you have a killer idea.

Most agents will expect to see a query letter. This should be a brief description of your project, why you are sending it to them, and why you think there's a market for it. Of course, the query letter should be cleanly typed and spell-checked. A sloppy presentation can ruin your chances of getting published.

Don't send a manuscript until it has been requested. When you do, always send a self-addressed stamped envelope to get your work returned. Remember, agents receive *thousands* of book submissions. Chances are they won't return your manuscript at their own cost.

INSIDE VIEW

"Make me laugh. Even if it's the best idea in the whole country, if your take isn't funny it won't work. The query should reflect your originality and sense of fun."

—JANE CAVELINA

HOW PUBLISHING HOUSES WORK

The first step is finding an editor who loves the project. The editor in turn must present it to other people at his publishing house. These include editorial, marketing, and sales personnel. The book has to be evaluated based on its content and sales potential. Even if your editor wants to do it, he has to have the support of the house to get the book accepted. Later on, the amount of enthusiasm the house has for the project will determine how much the company will promote your book.

Publishers produce a new list of books each season, but all titles are not publicized uniformly. The house does its own assessment of a book's sales potential. If the project is deemed highly commercial, it is likely to receive special treatment. This could mean a substantial budget for advertising, an author tour, and arrangements for talk show appearances, radio interviews, and magazine profiles.

In addition to the actual published book, there are other media in which the material may be used. Subsidiary rights sales are part of every book deal. As an author, you can profit from the sale of television adaptation rights, electronic and audio rights, and foreign, book club, and first and second serial rights. All of these will be bargaining points during your negotiating process. That's why you'll need a savvy agent. If the publisher retains all the rights or receives a percentage of the rights, your royalties will be reduced. In the beginning, a new writer won't be able to drive a hard bargain. Established authors whose work has a strong commercial appeal will be in a better negotiating position. In any case, an agent who knows the market and the publishing houses and understands your book's potential will be your best advocate.

THE EDITING PROCESS

To save a great deal of trouble and heartache when the editing process begins, you should have met with your editor prior to accepting an offer to see what changes he thinks are necessary. Get insight into how the editor sees the book, and decide how flexible you want to be. I have been very lucky in this regard. The editors I have worked with have helped me improve my work. This is not always the case. You may be asked to make changes you don't agree with or that you feel change the content of the piece in a way that destroys your voice. Getting a clear picture of what the editor wants should be part of the negotiation process. Don't agree and figure you'll fight it out later. You want to work with an editor who supports your project and is in sync with you and your style.

AGENTS

Having published my first book without an agent, I can say it's a mistake. Quite frankly, there's too much to figure out even if you do research. Ancillary rights clauses, royalty amounts, payback penalties—when it's time to sign a contract you'll find yourself lost in a sea of technical terminology. And remember, even if you submit directly to an editor who loves your work, his job is to make the best deal for his company. Agents deal with these issues on a daily basis and they're best equipped to handle them. If they've been in business for a number of years then they have established relationships with publishers and work using their own guidelines.

A talented agent will nurture your career, suggest projects, even introduce you to editors. There are also other issues to consider—the editorial process, the book design, and publicity. An agent will advise you on these issues so you're never in the position of fighting with your editor.

INSIDE VIEW

"It's all about the writing. If I fall in love with the writing, then I am able to make a very strong commitment to the author's career. That's what an agent should be about. They have to be involved for the long haul to nurture a writer's career, because you might not sell the first book. You may sell the second or the third, but if I can't be excited about someone's writing, how can I make a publisher feel that way?"

—BARBARA-J ZITWER

An agent's job is to get your work seen by the right people. The more contacts your agent has, the more your work will get seen and the more likely it will sell. Some agents may be able to get your material to just a few publishers; others can get you wide exposure. It is important to check out the reputation of any agent through your contacts in the business.

When interviewing with an agent, ask to speak to his other clients and get a detailed explanation of how he has worked with those clients. Try to get a sense of the agent's range of contacts with editors and how he handles negotiations and expenses. When speaking to the agent directly, ask how he intends to sell your book. Listen for concrete ideas that sound reasonable.

A good, ethical agent will do his job, take his commission, and behave professionally. But not all agents are ethical. Be wary of those who want long-term contracts, aren't specific about expenses, or charge reading fees. Any time an agent has this kind of control it can cost you—especially if you wish to terminate your contract.

LEGAL ISSUES

Even if you sign on with an agent you trust, have any legal agreement or contract reviewed by your attorney. Don't use your agent's attorney; find one whose only connection will be you.

It is always important to protect your work and yourself. Finished material should be copyrighted, and you will always need legal advice. Refer to Appendix IV for more information on copyright issues.

RESOURCES

Books

How to Write a Damn Good Novel by James N. Frey. $17.95. St. Martin's Press, 175 5th Avenue, New York NY 10010. A step-by-step, no-nonsense guide to dramatic storytelling.

Book Editors Talk to Writers by Judy Mandel. $12.95. John Wiley & Sons Inc., Professional Reference and Trade Group, 605 3rd Avenue, New York NY 10158-0012. Professional editors offer an insider's view of the world of book publishing.

The Insider's Guide to Book Editors, Publishers & Literary Agents by Jeff Herman. $19.95. Prima Publishing & Communications, P.O. Box 1260, Rocklin CA 95677.

The Art & Craft of Novel Writing by Oakley Hall. $17.95. Story Press, an imprint of F&W Publications Inc., 1507 Dana Avenue, Cincinnati OH 45207.

Directories

The Literary Market Place. R.R. Bowker, Reed Reference Publishing, 121 Chanlon Road, New Providence NJ

07974. A comprehensive directory of all publishers and agents, available at most libraries.

Periodicals
Publishers Weekly. 249 West 17th St., New York NY 10011. 800-278-2991. This is *the* guide to the publishing industry. Highlights market trends; reviews the new books in every category; offers insider news, interviews, and coverage of the best-sellers.

The New York Review of Books. Subscriber Service Dept., P.O. Box 420382, Palm Coast FL 32142-0382. 212-586-8003. An intellectual feast of reviews and essays by today's most influential writers.

The New York Times Book Review. A great source for keeping up with reviews of the important new books in the market.

Magazines
The Writer and *Writer's Digest.* Magazines that provide a variety of resources. They publish updates on markets, conferences, and other related topics. *The Writer,* 120 Boylston St., Boston MA 02116-4615. *Writer's Digest,* F&W Publications, 1507 Dana Avenue, Cincinnati OH 45207.

Organizations
American Society of Journalists and Authors, 1501 Broadway, Suite 302, New York NY 10036. Founded in

1948, the ASJA offers a variety of conferences, symposiums, and professional programs for the nonfiction writer. Members can be listed in the *Directory of Writers* and the Dial-A-Writer Referral Service, which helps connect writers to employment opportunities. The ASJA also offers members a newsletter covering a variety of issues relevant to the career of the nonfiction writer.

Chapter 6

Extra! Extra!:

Magazines and Newspapers

MASTHEAD

CHARLIE KADAU AND JOE RAIOLA
Associate Editors, *MAD* magazine

HARLAN COLLINS
Writer: "Today's Chuckle" syndicated column

LOIS ROSENTHAL
Editor, *Story* magazine

ALEX GREGORY AND PETER HUYCK
Senior Staff Writers, *Spy* magazine

NINA BELL ALLEN
Assistant Managing Editor, *Reader's Digest*

• • •

Of all the markets available to humor writers, magazines and newspapers are the easiest for talented people to enter. The sheer number of periodicals is staggering, even though the overall readership of print media is dwindling. A motivated comedy writer can submit work to a wide array of national magazines, local newspapers, trade magazines, and small-scale newsletters. Best of all, there is no need for agent representation. Do I seem overly enthusiastic? Is it obvious *I* started out here? I guess it is.

THE MARKET

Writers for magazines and newspapers can establish themselves by writing funny articles, short essays, or short stories. The tone and content of your work determines where you should direct your submissions. There are a number of humor-oriented magazines whose focus is satire and entertainment. Several women's magazines feature humorous essays and short stories. Most newspapers publish an occasional tongue-in-cheek feature or offbeat essay. You have the best chance of getting your work published if you submit wisely and appropriately.

The first step is to assess your writing style, goals, and flexibility. This will help you distinguish which publications are the best forums for your work.

HOW TO START

Without any credits, it's hard to get published in a major magazine or newspaper—not impossible, just difficult. If you have a great idea that seems appropriate for a major publication, write a query letter, call to find out the submission policy, and submit it accordingly, including a self-addressed, stamped envelope. The only way an editor can assess an unknown writer's work is by actually reading it. An intriguing letter might not be enough to persuade an editor to assign you an article. Initially, you may find that you have to write up the whole piece without a guarantee and compete against established contributors. Many writers are successful at this, but it's not necessarily the best strategy.

From my own experience, I would recommend developing a small portfolio of your articles to submit along with your query—and resume. It's unlikely that editors will read your writing samples, but they will see that your work has been validated by others. In my case, presenting myself as "semiestablished" meant that editors took my work very seriously. After reviewing my resume, one editor at a major magazine rejected my article idea but hired me to do a series of other pieces. The result was trips to New Orleans and Tucson and paychecks for four articles. Perception is important, and published clips will help you be perceived as a pro.

It's not a bad idea to begin by submitting to smaller publications. As a novice writer, you need learning experience. Interacting with editors and formatting a piece is tricky business. When I sold my first article, I remember sitting in the editor's office listening to her speak while thinking to myself, "When is she going to realize I don't have a clue about what she's saying?" But I listened and learned, and the result was a two-year relationship with a small magazine group, which led to work at bigger publications.

WHEN YOU SHOULD WORK FOR FREE

I hate to recommend this because it almost denies logic, but working for free helped me land my first big check from a magazine. By writing for a local newspaper, I was able to develop a large professional portfolio. When I used samples from my published work with my query letters, editors were assured I could do the job. Ironically, it was my hands-on experience writing for free that gave me the skill I needed when opportunities arose at major publications. Still, I caution beginning writers to make sure they are not being unfairly exploited. Working for free should only be done under the following conditions:

- The trade magazine or periodical is so small that even the staff members aren't drawing paychecks or are paid a minimum wage.
- You get an opportunity to write a piece that only a writer with considerable experience would normally have a chance to do.
- You need to develop your portfolio, gain expo-

sure to the market, and experience what it's like to work with an editor.

- It's an article that you absolutely love writing.

Your local newspaper and hobby or occupational periodicals are good places to get some experience even if some don't offer payment. Your "in" here could be that you share a location, hobby, or occupation with the readers, and your ideas will be of interest because of that common bond. It is also easiest to begin writing comedy about a subject you understand for an editor who has a relatively low-key approach. At small publications, editors are more accustomed to working with beginners, and the submission rate is less staggering than at high-profile publications. This guarantees that your work won't get lost in the slush pile.

INSIDE VIEW

"If you can get published in any circumstance possible, you have a beginning. You can then send clips out with your pitches. You need to have ammo. The way to have ammo is to think globally and act locally."

—HARLAN COLLINS

THINK BEFORE YOU SUBMIT

Whether you're interested in submitting to a small newsletter or a national magazine, the approach is the same. Read several issues of the publication to get a sense of the readership and editorial style. Pay special attention to the following factors:

- The cover: Note which articles are highlighted. These are the ones the editors feel will appeal most to their readers.
- The articles and regular features: Get a feeling for the range of subjects covered. Use some of these ideas as jumping-off points for writing parodies or comic takes on life.
- The editor's column: This will give you a sense of the overall philosophy of the magazine.
- The advertisements: These are the best indicators of the age, gender, and interests of the readership.
- Letters to the editor: Public response will not only help you gauge the market and readership, but the questions and concerns can be inspiration for articles and ideas.
- The humor pieces: Does your comedic style fit their image?

After you really get a sense of the magazine you want to pitch ideas to, start to think about what would be entertaining for its readers. Pieces that make fun of the magazine itself are not the best idea, as would be anything that disparages the readers. Start thinking of jokes, observations, or anecdotes that readers can relate to and identify with. For example, "The day the kids buried my clothes" might be a perfect fit for a parenting magazine, while "The crazy things people do to their engines during home repair" seems right for an automotive newsletter. These ideas would work within each periodical's format. The more you can identify the market, the more you will develop ideas that have a chance of being published.

When you move on to mainstream magazines and newspapers, your ideas will have to have a national scope. For example, "The Ice Cream Diet: What Susan Powter Doesn't Want You to Know" would be appropriate for a national woman's magazine because Ms. Powter is a well-known media figure. An article entitled "I Made a Million Collecting Bottles and Cans" would offer a humorous take on get-rich-quick plans that the whole country has seen publicized on infomercials.

COMEDY MAGAZINES

Comedy magazines such as *Spy*, *MAD*, and *Cracked* cover a wide array of topics, but each has a distinctive humor style. *MAD* and *Cracked*, for example, have a more youthful/bad-boy approach, while *Spy* is a bit more cutting-edge and sardonic. When submitting to these periodicals, make sure your style fits. Again, study recent issues to get a sense of the magazine's tone and content. And, of course, don't pitch an idea that was used only a few months ago.

The key really is to know the magazine market and editorial stance. It's a waste of time to send *Family Circle* a dark comic take on family fun at funerals or an essay satirizing politics. And, with few exceptions, never submit material that's overtly sexual in content or uses foul language. Comedy should come from your wit, not your ability to use expletives.

INSIDE VIEW

"*MAD* is a magazine of visual satire. So if someone can't draw, they should indicate in writing how to best present or carry through their idea."

—CHARLEY KADAU

NEWSPAPERS

It's harder to place your humor writing in newspapers because the market is usually dominated by syndicated columnists. Dave Barry and Erma Bombeck are the two most notable. If your style is similar to that of the paper's established contributors, you probably won't make a sale. Review the papers you are considering sending work to and assess if there is a place for your unique voice. As a rule, unknown writers don't find work as syndicated columnists. If, however, you develop a strong style of your own or write a column with a general-interest theme for a local paper, you may want to approach a syndication company with your body of work. For further information on this subject, read *Editor & Publisher* magazine, 11 West 19th St., New York NY 10011. Tel: 212-675-4380. You can also consult *The Editor & Publisher Syndicate Directory*, which provides resource material on all syndication companies.

In general, you will find humor writing in the style, living, and entertainment sections of newspapers. The best areas to focus on are largely known as "service" topics—parenting, cooking, dieting, dating, health, and fitness. A humorous take on a service article would parody the everyday concerns people have in these areas. For example, an article entitled "How to Make Up Dates to Keep Your Friends and Mother Happy" would offer funny tips for avoiding people who make you feel anxious about being single.

Newspapers often feature readers' contribution pages, where they publish funny anecdotes or stories about bizarre events. Even though these are short takes, they can still be useful additions to your portfolio, particularly if your material is well written. Good writing should always be your first priority. And, since comedy loves brevity, it's not how much you write, it's how you write it.

THE SHORT STORY

Writing a humorous short story is a distinctly different kind of challenge. *The New Yorker* and other literary publications occasionally feature a short story that's funny in an offbeat, subtle way. This kind of writing is difficult for a beginner. Even the mainstream magazines that feature short fiction—*Playboy* and *Cosmopolitan,* for example—require strong prose that is both sly and amusing.

If you survey the magazine market, you won't find a great number of comedic short stories being published. According to several editors I interviewed, it is almost impossible to find humorous short fiction. Few writers are skilled in this genre. If you are a gifted storyteller with a comedic yet literary style, there is a market for your work.

INSIDE VIEW

"In literary magazines humor is almost nonexistent, so when we find it we jump. People are influenced by television and write in a sitcom style where the humor is mean-spirited. We want someone like S. J. Perelman and Mark Twain, who can write about what is happening today in a sophisticated, intelligent way."

—LOIS ROSENTHAL

EDUCATION AND TRAINING

Journalism classes offer the best preparation for writing humor pieces for magazines and newspapers. These classes help you focus on being specific and guide you through the nuts and bolts of good journalistic writing. Most important, a journalism class will force you to write constantly. And the more you write, the more you improve your skills.

For the fiction writer, reading great literature is the best training for developing your comic voice. Certainly, if you want to enroll in a writing class, look for a program that champions the classics.

It's difficult for comedy writers to infiltrate the short story market and, therefore, feedback is hard to come by. This is a strong reason for taking classes or joining a writers' group. Feedback is important for your growth as a writer. It will help you experience how your work affects others.

INSIDE VIEW

"Education doesn't necessarily do it. It's the ability to write up the story, and you only get better by doing it over and over. You should figure out what you like reading, and that's what you should write. You also have to become a student of the magazine you wish to write for. Study the articles and see how many of the pieces are done by freelancers."

—PETER HUYCK

To succeed as a short story writer, you really have to become a fan of the medium. Read short stories in magazines as well as those published in collections and anthologies. Familiarize yourself with the market so you can direct your submissions accordingly. Reading short story periodicals and books also will keep you informed about conferences, workshops, seminars, contests, grants, and the people involved in the industry.

Formal classroom instruction must be supplemented with self-study. I urge you to read a great deal to keep yourself abreast of trends, news, and ideas. Anything that people are reading can be used as the basis for a humor piece. World events, trials, political happenings, and entertainment news are always choice topics for humorists.

SUBMITTING YOUR ARTICLE OR SHORT STORY

The submission process is fairly simple. Start by calling for submission guidelines. It is also important to find out the name and title of the editor who reviews the type of work you are submitting. Remember to include a self-addressed, stamped envelope, resume, and published writing samples. Attach a cover letter that describes your work in concise terms and explains why you feel it's right for the publication.

If you are not submitting a completed article, send a query letter that contains enough material to demonstrate your writing style and relay the idea behind your proposed article. With short-form humor, however, it is advisable to send a lengthy sample, if not the whole article.

As a novice short story writer, you must submit a completed work. A query, no matter how well written, can not fully reflect your storytelling ability. Editors interviewed for this section emphasized that in a humorous short story of publishable quality, the comedy must come from the characters, or from the situations the characters find themselves in. This can only be assessed by reading the whole story.

In general, editors prefer that you don't make multiple submissions. Writers do this all the time, but I suggest playing it safe and submitting to other publications only after getting a rejection. This is tough because it can take up to eight weeks to get a response, but you should pass the time writing, not waiting.

INSIDE VIEW

"You cannot be discouraged. You have to believe in yourself. There is rejection after rejection. You have to be able to handle it and learn from it. Louis L'Amour began his career with rejection after rejection. He began to look at that and grow as a writer."

—NINA BELL ALLEN

CONTRACTS

A magazine contract may look straightforward, but always have an attorney look it over. Of course this is not feasible if a local magazine or newspaper is paying $75 for your piece. Keep in mind that you should not sell your material outright. You sell a magazine one-time usage rights. In the long haul of your career you might be able to sell the rights to your article or short story to a collection or anthology. Contracts should feature what is known as a "kill fee." This is a small financial settlement paid to you if the periodical decides at some later point not to run your material.

From my own experiences, I have learned to be wary of those little magazines or newspapers that don't use contracts. As a beginner, you might agree to this because it's important to develop a portfolio. But without a contract, you might never get paid. Never agree to write a piece for a magazine with a sizable circulation when there is no contract involved.

RESOURCES

Magazines
The Writer, 120 Boylston St., Boston MA 02116-4615.
Writer's Digest, F&W Publications, 1507 Dana Avenue, Cincinnati OH 45207. Both offer detailed information on writing for periodicals.

Books

Freelancer and Staff Writer: Newspaper Features and Magazine Articles by William Rivers. $32.95. Wadsworth Publishing Company, 10 Davis Drive, Belmont CA 94002. Provides an inside view of the market and includes tips on how to figure out what editors want.

How to Be Successfully Published in Magazines by Linda Konner. $11.95. St. Martin's Press, 175 5th Avenue, New York NY 10010. The inside scoop on how to sell your work from top editors and successful magazine writers.

How to Write a Short Story by Sharon Sorenson. $8.00. Macmillan General Reference, a Prentice Hall Macmillan company, 15 Columbus Circle, New York NY 10023.

Directories

Two of the most comprehensive information guides about periodicals and magazines are *The Standard Periodical Directory,* Oxbridge Communications, 150 5th Avenue, Suite 302, New York NY 10011 and *The Gale Directory of Publications and Broadcast Media,* Gale Research, Inc., 835 Penobscot Bldg., Detroit MI 48226-4094.

Organizations

American Society of Journalists and Authors. 1501 Broadway, Suite 302, New York NY 10036. Founded in 1948, the ASJA offers a variety of conferences, symposiums, and professional programs for the nonfiction

143

writer. Members can be listed in the *Directory of Writers* and *Dial-A-Writer* referral services, which help connect writers to possible employment opportunities. The ASJA newsletter covers a variety of topics of interest to the nonfiction writer.

Chapter 7

The Radio Roundup:

Short-Form Radio Comedy

"Radio comedy is theater of the mind. The listener is visualizing it funnier than we could write it."

—PAUL HOOPER

RADIO ROUNDUP CALL

MARC CHASE
Program Director, WEBN Cincinnati

TODD CUMMINGS
Creative Director, American Comedy Network

PAUL HOOPER
Creative Director, Bug Bytes Comedy

TONY NOVIA
Editor, Contemporary Hit Radio, *R&R Magazine*

JOEL PERRY
Producer/Writer, Cutler Comedy

• • •

Imagine a job where you get to write jokes, and get paid for them, and never be criticized. Great, huh? Of all the professional comedy writing I've done, submitting to the ABC Radio Networks Comedy Service was the most satisfying. Of course, there is a downside. Radio comedy services only pay for what they buy. If you submit ten pieces, you may only receive payment for one. At $25–75 a pitch, it doesn't seem like much money. In the beginning, it certainly won't be. But the longer you do it, the better you will get. At the same time, you'll build your relationships with the comedy services you work for. There are several established radio comedy services, but if you are a beginner you'll probably stand a better chance at selling your material to new companies that don't have an established roster of writers. Your first step is to learn about the radio market.

Writing for this market requires that you become a student of radio. Familiarize yourself with the format of comedy in this medium. Once you become comfortable with the style and format of comedy writing for radio, it's time to employ the most important writer's affirmation: Write, write, write to improve your craft. Submitting to radio is a numbers game. If various contributors from around the country are submitting all at the same time, it is likely that much of the material will be similar. It is your job to get there first and be funnier.

THE MARKET

Morning and evening rush-hour shows are the biggest broadcasters of short-form comedy. To avoid having stations in the same cities using identical material, each comedy service company serves only one station in the same area. This creates a situation where several comedy services can be working in each market. Although it appears that radio DJs write all their own material, it is not the case. While they do prepare some comedy material on their own, often it is supplemented by a comedy service. Services supply finished comedy bits on tape for the DJs to play on their shows. In addition, services may supply scripts for DJs to read, or a combination tape and script so the DJ can interact on air within a comedy sketch. Since there are a wide variety of radio formats—rock, country, R&B, Christian—each service creates material it believes the client will want for a specific audience. For example, a comedy service would not send a piece containing sexual innuendoes to a Christian music station. Nor would they submit a bit of political satire to a heavy metal channel. It's your responsibility to listen to the radio—and I mean *all* the channels. You may not like the music, but if the comedy is similar to the material you write, you may want to focus on that station. It is also important to gauge how the DJs are performing the comedy. This will help you understand how to prepare your own material.

In addition to listening to the radio, it is important that you keep an eye on the music business as a whole. Determine which bands or performers are getting airplay. You'll be writing for the same group of listeners. It is necessary for you to read *R&R Magazine*. This is the industry trade journal that follows the trends, personalities, and daily business of radio industry. The magazine also publishes a yearly ratings report and directory resource guide, which includes lists of all the radio comedy services that you'll want to submit to. To receive a copy of the directory or to subscribe to the trade magazine, contact Radio and Records Inc., 1930 Century Park West, Los Angeles CA 90067.

INSIDE VIEW

"The market is glutted with comedy. It's the rock-and-roll franchise of the 1990's. At each service there's an inherent style that develops over time. When reviewing submissions, I don't criticize material for being good, bad, or indifferent. It's about whether it works for our style. A guy who's a *Home Improvement* comedy writer is not going to write for *Seinfeld*. A writer can submit to each comedy service and see where their style fits."

—TODD CUMMINGS

HOW TO START

After paying a great deal of attention to the style of radio comedy, you should familiarize yourself with the joke format. Parodies of commercials, movies, music, and celebrities are the most popular formats. These are usually 30 to 60 seconds long and must spoof some known entity or celebrity in the public arena (e.g., the Roseanne Candy Barr, Pope Tarts, or Forrest Sawyer Gump, the idiot newscaster).

Another favorite format is the interactive dialogue. The comedy service supplies a script and a recording of someone imitating a famous person. The idea is that it will appear as if the DJ is actually talking with the celebrity.

Radio stations also favor comedy bits that are written so the station's call letters are the punch lines. Call letters are the station's identification code—for example, WABC Radio in New York. A comedy bit incorporating a station's call letters is referred to as a call-letter drop and it should last for 15 seconds or less.

Here are two examples of call-letter drops:

Voice-over: *MMM good, mmm good, that's what WXYZ is, mmm good!* or

Voice-over of someone who sounds scared: *I was sound asleep when suddenly I was shocked into a hellish reality. I had to go to work!*

Announcer voice-over: *WXYZ. We'll wake you up because you're not at Mom's house anymore.*

149

EDUCATION AND TRAINING

As discussed in previous chapters, any classroom work you do should focus on writing comedic bits and help you hone your ability to find humor in everyday events. In general, the best places to learn these skills are stand-up and improvisation classes.

WHAT YOU SHOULD KNOW

If movies are a visual art form, radio is an audio art form. Given that, your script should capitalize on familiar voices and sound effects. Any sound that the listener can readily identify helps clarify the premise of the piece. At around 30 seconds a bit, there's not a great deal of time for a setup. If a segment begins with a William Shatner sound-alike, the listener is already oriented to the piece. In doing parodies, it is important to consider which audio cues will help the listener imagine what's coming. For example, if your material is a parody of a television show, you would want to stipulate in your script that theme music from the show would be used. You have to pay attention to the details of sound, since that is how the audience experiences comedy on the radio.

From my own experience, I can emphatically state that in order to sell your material you have to anticipate the needs of the service. Immediacy is a major factor to consider. If your material comments on recent news events, you need to submit quickly. If you can write fast and hook up to a comedy service via fax or a special phone line, you'll be able to cash in on your ideas. If the comedy service specializes in produced material that is not necessarily time-sensitive, you have more leeway. For instance, immediacy is not an issue in submitting parodies of vintage movies, TV shows, commercials, or sketches about dating, marriage, or school. This kind of material should be short, and the setup has to be strong. For example, a bit could open with the theme from *Oprah* and a voice-over stating, "Today on Oprah, guests victimized by appearing on Geraldo." Here's another example of a strong setup: "In this month's

Cosmopolitan, 'A diet to eat men by.' " With a bit of creativity, the possibilities are endless.

BREAKING IN

You don't need agent representation to break into the radio market, so it's all up to you. First review the listings of comedy services in the *R&R* directory and in trade magazines. Call each service to find out submission procedures. Some companies will give you script format guidelines. Other services will ask you to call your work in. These instructions are easy enough to follow. If, however, a service or station does not offer guidelines, the basics apply—your script should be double spaced, typed in traditional script format on nice white paper. Include these abbreviations: VO for voice-over, SFX for sound effects.

The submission procedure will indicate whether the service is looking for topical material or material with a longer shelf life. Also inquire about which radio formats the service sells to and if its clients include a station in your area. Once you determine the format and get a sense of who your potential listeners are, you can begin to pitch material.

It's difficult to pitch to two services simultaneously, because they both may wind up using your material and you may not find out about the purchases until after the piece has been produced. That is why it is important to ask about how long you should wait to find out if you have made a sale. Services will only call you when they want to buy something. They get too many submissions to call everyone whose work they reject. Realize that given the topical nature of most of the material you write, you will only have one shot. After that, your jokes will be too dated to sell elsewhere.

If you fail to make at least one sale after many months of submitting, you should reevaluate your work or the service you are submitting to. Listen to the station that the service sells to in your area. Does your material fit the station's style? Are your ideas close to what it is doing? If not, you may have to revamp your style or submit to another comedy service. If you find that you are continually submitting topical ideas, and you are getting your material in too late, it's time to move on to a service that's less competitive.

LOCAL STATIONS

Radio is everywhere. You'd be surprised how many smaller stations are interested in buying polished material directly from a writer. Smaller stations do not have the money to retain comedy services or produce their own in-house material. Some major stations also buy directly from writers, especially if the material is extremely funny or cutting-edge.

In both these situations, call the program manager's office to find out if the station accepts unsolicited material. At first you may not be offered money for your material, but if the station begins to use your ideas consistently, it's time to negotiate or move on.

Poll everyone you know to determine if anyone has contacts working for radio stations. This could be your "in." When you submit, make sure your material is top-notch. This initial contact is your calling card.

INSIDE VIEW

"Most people who work at radio stations usually started by hanging out at them. Radio is a lifestyle."

—MARC CHASE

Chapter 8

Thinking of You:

The Greeting Card Industry

HOUSE OF CARDS

RICK HAMILTON
Senior Creative Director, American Greetings

MILTON KRISTT
Editor and Publisher, *Greetings* magazine

MARIANNE MCDERMOTT
Executive Vice President, Greeting Card Association

ANGIE NOVAK
National Sales Manager, Paper Moon Graphics

MARILYN MOORE
Director of Publishing, C.R. Gibson Greeting Cards

•   •   •

Have you ever lost track of time chuckling over humorous greeting cards in a stationery store? Probably everyone has. I bet you haven't considered what a great market this could be for a joke writer. Much like short-form radio comedy, the greeting card business is the ideal market for the witty gag specialist. A humorous card consists of a visual cue with a comic setup on the front and a punch line inside. Is this the right market for you? Since you may be considering it for the first time, let's study the basics.

THE MARKET

The greeting card business is booming. There are hundreds of companies selling millions of cards every year. This boom brings with it a high demand for writers. A majority of these companies use freelancers, and they're especially looking for writers who can create a gag for a specific occasion. In fact, all the greeting card executives I interviewed for this book said that while they have plenty of writers for their sentimental card lines, they are always looking for humor writers. This demand makes submitting work easier, but the competition is tough. Companies reject 90% of what they receive. Unlike in other markets, however, creative directors and their staff review all the submissions. Easy submission policies and a guaranteed read—it doesn't get better than that. It is important to know that women buy a majority of greeting cards, and since the customer base is diverse, your comedy must have a wide appeal.

HOW TO START

Hit the card racks. There is no better way to learn the market than to see how it's presented to the public. Your mission here is twofold: you need to study how comedy is utilized in a card, and to learn to recognize the distinctive style and tone of each company.

Can you blend writing with a visual image and, in just a few sentences, acknowledge an occasion and put a smile on a customer's face? Only one way to tell. Write!

INSIDE VIEW

"The most significant aspect is that the writing be occasion-specific. There are writers who can write, but the lines may not be appropriate for the giving situation. The message has to be what the giver wants to say to the receiver."

—MARILYN MOORE

First, select an occasion. The next step is up to you. If you are a visual person, you may want to work with a particular visual image in mind. Don't worry, you don't have to draw. You can work from a visual image you have in your head. Write down a description of the image and save it. If you have trouble creating your own, take a visual idea from a magazine, art book or photograph. Now, focusing on the occasion and the image, write a series of setups and punch lines. Do this in the same way you write short-form humor. Utilize puns, word play, metaphor, what-ifs, parody, even satire. Write down whatever strikes you as funny. After you have assembled your material, edit out those pieces that just don't work or are too clumsy. The remaining material should then be refined until it is both funny and concise enough to sell as a greeting card. Remember to submit your visual material along with your writing sample.

INSIDE VIEW

"We are all freelance-written, so we encourage submissions. I personally look through all the mail. I am more apt to notice a writer who submits the work with a visual even if it's a stock photo we wouldn't use. It helps to present the overall concept."

—ANGIE NOVAK

If you find that starting with a visual image is not comfortable, follow your normal joke-writing routine. I like to start with a blank pad. Select an occasion and jot down all the aspects of the occasion you can think of. Get all the information onto the pad; then start experimenting with puns, word play, sounds, and meanings. Take the straight facts and play with them until they're funny. Now that you are in a writing mode, head back to the card racks. Given what you've written, review the style of each company and see which you're drawn to. Jot down the names of those companies. These will be the places you'll submit to first.

Inside View

"The smart thing to do for anyone getting into the business is to learn what each card company does. They should not waste their time sending beautiful pictures of bunnies and flowers to a company that does tongue-in-cheek graphics. A good 60% of submissions are not appropriate. I still get cards of male nudes even though our company hasn't done beefcake since 1980."

—ANGIE NOVAK

EDUCATION AND TRAINING

As you analyze humorous greeting cards, note the economy of words. Comedy loves brevity, and given the size of the greeting card, what choice is there? Even on cards that are more text-driven (such as greeting cards that are designed as little books), the text still consists of a series of short takes. You have to study to become a sharp wordsmith. Certainly, traditional education is beneficial, but I would also suggest taking a variety of classes in which learning about word play, brevity and/or putting a funny spin on daily events are the goals. Here are a few options:

- Copywriting class: Ad lines do exactly what cards do. In a couple of sentences, ads present information in an eye-catching way.
- Poetry class: Not every card has to rhyme, but learning a sense of rhythm and meter can be useful in all types of humor.
- Improvisation and stand-up classes: These courses help you find your comedic voice and force you to look for ideas and inspiration in the issues of daily life.

Should you take these classes just to write greeting cards? No. You should take these classes because they will help you improve your short-form comedy writing for every market, as will reading books and magazines, keeping up with the news, and knowing what's hot in movies and television and the music business. You must keep in touch with what America is talking and laughing about. Since your goal is to become a wordsmith, I would suggest also reading comedic quotation anthologies, short-form humor books, and toastmaster speech collections found in the general reference section of your local library.

INSIDE VIEW

"We are aggressively seeking comedy illustra-
tors and writers. Forget all the cliches. We want
fresh stuff—the next Gary Larson. We're looking for unique people who can highlight an occasion with a point of view."

—RICK HAMILTON

SUBMITTING

The submission process is consistent throughout the
greeting card business. Call and inquire if the company
uses freelancers. If they do, they will send you a guideline sheet and/or a release form. The guideline sheet will
give you an insight into what the company wants and
how your material should be laid out. To submit material without reviewing this would be a waste of their time
and yours. Any company that requires a release form will
not review your work without it. Given the number of
submissions that each company receives, duplications are
bound to happen. This is why most companies ask you
to sign the release form.

You can use 3-x-5 index cards to present your material. On one side of a card, write the setup. Use the
other side for the gag. It is also a good idea to label each
card with your name and address. Some companies may

ask you not to do that, while others will ask you to also include your social security number. This is to make it easier for them to locate you should the cards become separated from your submission packet. If you have worked with a visual image that you have either described or taken from another medium, remember to include it. The company will not use a visual image that is copyrighted elsewhere, but they will design their own. Remember, your material will sell itself. Don't spend valuable time writing a snappy pitch letter. Focus your creative energy on writing your cards.

INSIDE VIEW

"Sometimes you receive something from people who say, 'This is unlike any other greeting card you have ever had.' This implies that there is something wrong with what *we* have and there is a need for something different. The people in the industry don't think there's anything wrong with what they're doing, or they wouldn't publish it."

—MARILYN MOORE

Allow six to eight weeks for a response, and of course always include a self-addressed, stamped envelope for your work to be returned to you. You can expect anywhere from $50 to $150 a card, the higher end being reserved for those who sell to the company consistently.

There are no contracts, no agents, and, unfortunately, no royalties. Greeting cards are usually a buyout. This is not optimal, but given the format and the time involved, it's good compensation.

INSIDE VIEW

"In our company we will pay higher if we have a real need or if a person's a real resource who should be nurtured and we think we can build a card line around them."

—MARILYN MOORE

STATIONERY SHOWS

For a broad overview of the business, I'd suggest attending stationery shows. These occur around the country at different times, and you can usually find out about them by reading the industry trade magazine *Greetings*.

At a stationery show, companies present their product lines in booths that look like little retail shops. If you find a company whose work you are particularly drawn to, speak to the employees informally. Do not, however, strike up a conversation when they are busy with customers. If the staff is free and willing to talk about the company and what they're looking for, get all of the information that you can. It is not always wise to pull out a portfolio unless they ask to see your work. You can always submit your work later and state that you spoke to them at the show. Keep in mind that at a stationery show the employees have another agenda—selling their products. As you walk around the stationery show, you will get a general feeling for just how large the market is.

RESOURCES

The Greeting Card Industry Directory. $60.00. The Greeting Card Association, 1200 G Street N.W., Suite 760, Washington DC 20005. Tel: 202-393-0336. This biannual directory lists the names, locations, products and key personnel of over 1,000 greeting card publishers and suppliers.

Greetings Magazine Buyers Guide. $29.00—but free with a subscription to *Greetings* magazine, Mackay Publishing, 307 5th Avenue, New York NY 10016. Tel: 212-679-6677. This directory provides information on greeting card publishers, manufacturers, distributors, and the industry in general. *Greetings* magazine, a retailer-oriented monthly magazine, offers interviews with key players in the industry and reports on trends in sales and products.

How to Write and Sell Greeting Cards by Molly Wigand. $15.95. Writer's Digest Books, F&W Publications, 1507 Dana Avenue, Cincinnati OH 45207. A complete overview of the greeting card business for the writer.

Chapter 9

Comedy, Inc.:

Writing Corporate Communications

THE COMEDY EXECUTIVES

MARY CLAIRE COLLINS
    Clients: Kraft General Foods, Allstate, Ameritech, FMC Corporation, Zurich-America Insurance Group, Citicorp, CNA Insurance, Chicago's Metro Transit System, Price Waterhouse, Vanguard Construction, Motivation Media, Inc., Whirlpool, and Blue Cross/Blue Shield of Illinois.
    Author: *How to Make Money Writing Corporate Communications*

JOEL GOODMAN
    Clients: AT&T, Ben and Jerry's, Cornell University, du Pont, Mobil Oil, 3M Company, United Cerebral Palsy, YMCA, and Ziff-Davis
    Director and Founder, The Humor Project, Inc.
    Author: *Laugh Affirmations: 1001 Ways to Add Humor to Your Life*
    Editor: *Laughing Matters* magazine

CAROL SCHINDLER
    Clients: American Express, Coach Leatherware, du Pont, Federal Express, Ford, IBM, MTV, Sandoz, and Toshiba
    Performer: HBO Encyclopedia, founding member of Chicago City Limits Improvisation Company

Tony Taddei
Clients: AT&T, Con Edison, Johnson & Johnson, New York Telephone, New Jersey Bell, Pathmark Supermarkets, Sears, and Sony

Pam Woodroff
Clients: IBM, Mary Kay Cosmetics, Pfizer, Squibb, and Rubbermaid
Writer, performer, and teacher, Gotham City Improv

• • •

In the same way that writers fine-tune their comic voices to fit a specific magazine readership or television audience, writing comedy for corporate clients requires a writer to cultivate a certain sensibility. This is a challenging market that should be pursued only by fairly experienced writers. Remember, corporate America expects a certain level of professionalism.

THE MARKET

The basic need of any company is to be able to communicate to its employees, market representatives, sales force, and public. Humor can be used in a variety of situations—speeches, presentations, newsletters, and ad campaigns. But the ultimate goal is always the same: Get the message across.

Corporate communications can not include references to politics, religion, profanity, sexuality, racism, sexism, age discrimination, or any point of view that may be offensive. Writers who begin working in this area are at first mortified by the editing process. Corporate communications are meant to inform, not provoke or shock.

INSIDE VIEW

"The material can't be funny for the sake of being funny, or the message gets lost. Things are funny because the business audience relates to the everyday work situations, the company jargon, and familiar names."

—CAROL SCHINDLER

The point of corporate writing is to make the company, the employees, or the product look good. Communicating with humor boosts morale, reinforces team spirit, and presents information in an upbeat way. Effective corporate writing can accomplish the following goals:

- Create enthusiasm for the sale of a new product.
- Boost morale after downsizing, a corporate takeover, or a substantial change in the company structure.
- Train employees in a new business method, or inform them of a corporate mission.
- Celebrate a corporate success.
- Zip up a speech for a corporate executive, trainer, or special presenter.
- Help lure buyers at trade shows.

The sensitive nature of business, however, makes corporate executives proceed with caution when it comes to humor. Considering the state of comedy writing today, this is not surprising. Raw, shocking material and mean-spirited jokes would make company executives uncomfortable. Writers need to assure executives of their ability to tone down humor and accommodate the corporate structure. When meeting with a corporate client, writers must realize they're seeking work in the business world and must comply with the company style.

If you want to write for corporate clients, cultivate a professional decorum. Keep the funny stuff on the page and present your product. This is what executives understand. They might laugh at an outlandishly dressed high-energy comic, but they probably wouldn't hire him. The reason is simple. For the time period that the writer is employed and the material is used, the writer represents that company and the executive who hired him. Can you become part of a company? That's what you have to ask yourself. You must take into account the restrictions, conservatism, hierarchy, and other aspects of corporate culture.

The best advice I can offer is what I have learned through working in a variety of media. Every market has its limitations in the way material can be presented. I never view this as a stumbling block, because I know these limitations can actually promote creativity. The fact that corporate America is an entity unto itself will actually work in your favor. Comedy always works best when it presents experiences the audience can relate to. The world of business focuses on products and services, selling, and company rules. Your material will be based on these different elements and it should engage everyone who works for the company because it highlights their shared experiences. Corporate comedy writing has its restrictions, but it's lucrative work if you can get it. With an average day rate of $300 to $750 it is a pretty enticing market.

INSIDE VIEW

"You have to be very specific about what you can do for the company. You want to clarify that comedy has a target—the message the company wants to give out. It can't be silly or nonsensical because the point is communication. It has to come from the people in the company, what their day entails, and the challenges they face."

—TONY TADDEI

FORMATS FOR CORPORATE WRITING

Corporate writing serves to reinforce or highlight a point the company wants to make, teach its employees, or just break up the monotony of a day of presentations. But no company is going to lighten up a sales meeting with a three-hour vaudeville romp. Your humor writing should help convey a message, not obscure it. Following are ways to inject humor into corporate situations:

- Jokes to highlight key points of a speech or presentation. Examples might include: "How not to approach a client" or "Why company X can't keep up with us."
- Humorous sketches that demonstrate product use or sales technique, but not in a manner that makes fun of the product.
- Song parodies that use familiar tunes with clever, funny lyrics.
- Phony guest speakers set up a discussion. Their presentation starts out very reasonably, then turns into a spoof. The employees slowly realize they're being had and enjoy the proceedings.

INSIDE VIEW

"Anyone involved in communication can appreciate incorporating humor into business. For the humor to work it should accomplish one or more of the following: relationship building, helping people work together, stress management, and focusing them on their creativity."

—JOEL GOODMAN

Your material may be performed live, or as part of a video presentation, depending on the company's budget. If it is a full-scale show, or what is commonly referred to as an "industrial," production companies heading the project will hire writers, performers, designers, and a director.

HOW TO START

The corporate writer already should have some experience and training in working on short-form comedy. The first step is familiarizing yourself with the language of business. Read *The Wall Street Journal,* the business section of *The New York Times, Forbes, Business Week,* or *The Economist.* After a few weeks of reading general business magazines, you'll be able to detect the rhythm of business-speak. You should also familiarize yourself with companies and trends that are hot and the changing face of corporate America.

After this initial preparation, you have to figure out where the opportunities lie. You have two options: Either find a lead through your network of contacts, or cold call.

Networking with other writers and performers is the best way in. The people you meet at comedy clubs, writers' classes, and writers' groups will be knowledgeable about working in the field of corporate communications. Some may work regularly for a production company that creates material for the market. Your entry into the business will depend on the caliber of your work. Your contacts will recommend you if they are impressed by your writing skills and experience. Ask to see material they have written for corporate clients.

If you do not live in a place where there are networking possibilities, your method of starting will involve pitching to industrial producers or companies directly. This is tough to do if you don't have corporate writing experience. Inevitably you'll be asked to submit a portfolio. But how do you acquire a portfolio if you have no working experience? You can create dummy material, but the best idea is to offer your services—usually for free—to a nonprofit agency. Familiarize yourself with nonprofit organizations by examining the materials they send out, the events they hold, and their media presence. Analyze these things to see where your humor writing would fit in.

A cold call to a company should begin with getting information from the company phone operator or receptionist. Inquire who at the company is responsible for meeting planning, sales conferences, and/or staff training. Depending on the size of the company, these jobs may involve one or several people. If there is one central contact, you might want to try to prepare a submission that includes samples of each different type of work you have done. If you must contact a few people in charge of different departments, you will want to tailor your writing samples to their specific areas. The next step involves calling each contact's office directly. When the secretary or assistant answers the phone, ask for his or her name. It is important to form a relationship with these support people. Explain to the secretary or assistant exactly what you want to do, and inquire about the use of freelancers. Usually they can tell you whether they use only in-house people or a select group of outside media planners. If they use an outside group, get the name and number of that group and contact them for possible work. If they use freelancers, ask the secretary or assistant how you should submit your work.

Should an assistant or secretary prove unhelpful, you may want to contact an executive directly. If you are able to get him or her on the phone, keep it brief. Explain what you do and how your work could be helpful to the company. Ask for an opportunity to meet or submit your portfolio. Some executives will not want to stay on the phone for longer than a few seconds. If this is the case, ask if you can submit your portfolio with a letter explaining your interest.

To put your best foot forward, you should learn everything you can about the company before meeting with anyone. Publicly listed companies publish annual reports, which can be found in the library. You can also use the computer index at the library to look up mainstream and trade magazine articles published about that company. Use your connections to get copies of company newsletters, brochures, and other printed material. All of these factors will be helpful when you make your pitch. You want to be clear about your ability to focus on the company's products or services, train its staff, and create a more productive work environment.

At a meeting or in your written presentation, give specific examples of the type of humor that you feel is appropriate and useful for private industry. You not only have to educate the executives about the possibilities, but you must reassure them. Don't expect that a vague description is enough to help them to envision your comedic sensibility. These are corporate executives, not filmmakers.

INSIDE VIEW

"Executives consider and treat the creative person as being different. You have to learn to talk the talk and walk the walk so they can be comfortable with you."

—CAROL SCHINDLER

Remember, your work is your calling card. The presentation must be crisp and businesslike. It should reflect your sense of professionalism and clearly demonstrate your writing skills.

INSIDE VIEW

"The marketing packet of your pitch must look very professional and demonstrate that you understand corporate structure. You have to appeal to their way of life. Even if you are unconventional, they want to know that you understand how to communicate like them."

—MARY CLAIRE COLLINS

The work you do as an independent freelancer will be on a small scale—writing jokes for speeches, sketches for small presentations, or material for newsletters. When working for a production company, you are part of a team. The proposals for these kinds of pitches are quite elaborate and costly, as are the actual events that are produced. These "industrials" involve performers, sets, and costumes. Whether you work as an independent or as part of the creative team of an industrial, remember that you are providing a service and your goal is pleasing the client.

In the beginning, working on small projects by yourself or larger projects with established production companies will provide you with a manageable workload. If this proves to be the right market for you, you can work your way up to producing industrials, as many of the writers interviewed here have done.

GETTING THE JOB DONE

Once you are hired as an independent or part of a creative team, your first chore is to get the inside scoop on company products, jargon, competitors, triumphs, and so forth. You will weave this information into your writing, and the recognition factor will add an extra dimension to the presentation.

During the information-gathering process, you have to remember you're dealing with business people. You must approach them in a manner that makes them feel comfortable. Review what you have learned with them and carefully recap the guidelines for the project. This will assure the corporate executives that your goal is to promote the best interest of the company and foster team spirit. They'll be more likely to give information if they know you'll use it positively.

INSIDE VIEW

"The biggest mistake I've seen creative people make was that they were not accommodating in having someone edit their work. This is out of the question in the corporate world. The people who hire you could lose their jobs if they allow the wrong message to be presented."

—MARY CLAIRE COLLINS

You also can learn a great deal about the company by making site visits, seeing how and where it markets its services and goods, and shadowing an employee during a weekday. Raise these ideas with the executive who hired you. Get an official approval before you start your field work.

NEGOTIATING YOUR FEE

If you are hired by a big production company, your fee and payment schedule may already be decided. If you are working as an independent, you'll have to negotiate your fee with the corporation. This is business, not plea bargaining. You have to have confidence. Think about it: Would you hire someone to represent your company who appeared disorganized, unsure, or anxious? You have to negotiate for compensation and expenses. You can charge an hourly rate for an independent project, or you might want to consider charging ten percent of the overall budget. You may initially want to ask for a bit more than you think you should get, just so there's room for bargaining. If, however, several people are bidding on the job, you want your price to be as reasonable as possible.

Negotiating fees is tough. There is no union, and you have to establish a day rate. A figure of $300–$400 is fair, but consider charging less if you are starting out. Contracts are often verbal, but it's preferable to draw up a letter in which you negotiate a third of the money up front and final payment thirty days later.

In addition to ironing out payment issues, you should review due dates, how much material is needed, and submission dates, and find out who will grant you the final okay in terms of payment. The more you work out now, the less trouble you'll have later.

RESOURCES

Books
Directory of Corporate Meeting Planners. $337.00. Reed Reference Publishing, P.O. Box 31, New Providence NJ

07974. Tel: 800-521-8110. With listings of over 17,500 corporate meeting planners, this is a comprehensive guide to the industry's key players whose clients are among the biggest corporations in America.

Corporate Script Writing, A Professional's Guide by Ray Di Zazzo. $34.95. Focal Press, Butterworth-Heineman, 80 Montvale Avenue, Stoneham MA 02180. Explains the basic rules of corporate script writing and what to expect when working with producers and directors.

How to Make Money Writing Corporate Communications by Mary Claire Collins. $12.00. A Perigee book, published by The Berkley Publishing Group, 200 Madison Avenue, New York NY 10016. This how-to book is concise and well organized. The section on cold calling is especially helpful.

Error-Free Writing, A Lifetime Guide to Flawless Business Writing by Robin A. Cormier. $14.95. Prentice-Hall Career and Personal Development, Englewood Cliffs NJ 07632.

Organizations

The Humor Project. 110 Spring Street, Saratoga Springs NY 12866. Tel: 518-587-8770. Run by humor writer Joel Goodman, this group provides information on utilizing humor in business settings, schools, and organizations. The group features conferences, a catalog of books, games and videos, and a newsletter called "Laughing Matters."

The International Association of Business Communicators, 1 Hallidie Plaza, Suite 600, San Francisco CA 94102. Tel: 415-433-3400. The IABC provides information and seminar referrals on corporate communication topics.

Chapter 10
A Final Word

In closing, I have to relate an incident that occurred while I was writing this book. A neighbor who had studied photography was looking for work. Although she was not a writer, I decided to try my pragmatic approach on her. I told her that the National Stationery Show was a few weeks away and that photography was often featured on greeting cards. To really get a sense of the market, I explained that she should attend the show, figure out which companies used photography in their product lines, and make contacts.

I told her that she could probably get in by paying a visitor's fee, but if she polled her friends and family she could find someone in a related business whose card she could use to get in free of charge.

My neighbor was a very good student. She studied the market, got a sense of the products that sold, and, armed with the business card of an aunt and uncle who own a stationery store in Florida, attended the National Stationery Show in New York. The result—her first sale. She is ecstatic, and I have a feeling that her first sale will lead to the first sale of my book—to her.

Information about the business is as important to success as talent. Even the most brilliant novel ever written will remain unread if the writer doesn't have a clue of how to get it to an editor, secure representation, and have the book published. Do your homework. Immerse yourself in the market you select, and *write*!

When I was starting out, there were a number of books and periodicals that were not only informative, but inspirational. I advise you to read them:

Books

The Comic Toolbox—How to Be Funny Even If You're Not by John Vorhaus. $14.95. Silman-James Press, distributed by Samuel French, Inc., 7623 Sunset Blvd., Hollywood CA 90046.

Creating Unforgettable Characters by Linda Seger. $12.95. An Owl book. Henry Holt & Company, 115 W. l8th St., New York NY 10011.

Wild Mind—Living the Writer's Life by Natalie Goldberg. $10.95. A Bantam New Age book. Bantam Books, 1540 Broadway, New York NY 10036.

Writing Down the Bones—Freeing the Writer Within by Natalie Goldberg. $10.00. Shambhala Publications, Horticulture Hall, 300 Massachusetts Avenue, Boston MA 02115.

The No Experience Necessary Writer's Course by Scott Edelstein. $10.95. Scarborough House/Publishers, Chelsea MI 48118.

Secrets of a Freelance Writer by Robert W. Bly. $10.95. An Owl book. Henry Holt & Company, 115 W. 18th St., New York NY 10011.

Magazines
The Writer, 120 Boylston St., Boston MA 02116-4615. *Writer's Digest,* F&W Publications, 1507 Dana Avenue, Cincinnati OH 45207. Both offer insight into markets and developing the craft of writing. These magazines are also filled with information about contests, schools, and conferences.

Agents and Managers

Every writer I meet wants to be represented by an important Hollywood or New York agent, but when I ask them why, I realize how little they know about what an agent should do and how he goes about his job. Agents and managers can be career makers, resources for project ideas, or lethargic leeches. How do you separate the good agents from the bad ones? Most times you can't, at least not right away. Do your homework.

In each chapter I suggest that you read the trades, and network in the industry; get to know people and their reputations. If you have been doing this, you probably have a sense of who are the ethical representatives. How do you find a reputable agent or manager? Use this screening process:

- Approach writing organizations, authors, entertainment lawyers, and other professionals you come in contact with through your work. Even before you actually acquire an agent, begin to learn about which agents and managers are seen as honest and well connected.

- If you don't have a specific agent in mind, consult the agent listings in the Hollywood Creative Directory and the Literary Market Place. If you find an agent who is open to taking on a newcomer, use your contacts to find out more about his reputation.
- When possible, before hiring an agent or manager speak to several other clients and ask about the agent or manager's business style. This should be done through contacts you have, not the people the agent or manager refers to you. Obviously, if an agent were to give you a name it would be someone who may not be able to offer an unbiased opinion.
- Be led by your brain, not your ego. If an agent wants to represent you without first seeing your written work, then he's a lousy agent. It's common sense. How could an agent work with you if he doesn't know how you write?

I was able to find an agent through people I knew. A social worker friend hooked me up to his school chum, who was representing television writers. On another occasion, a casting director made calls on my behalf to several television agents with whom she had worked. Ironically enough, I made my first sale to a cable station through a commercial agent who saw me perform my stand-up routine in a comedy club. The agent decided I was the wrong type for acting in commercials, but pitched my work for writing jobs.

The roles of an agent and personal manager can overlap. But, in general, an agent's job is to submit your work and negotiate deals. Personal managers may also find you work, but they act primarily as business managers, overseeing all the aspects of your career including financial planning. You can expect to pay your agent and manager 10%–15% apiece. Is losing up to 30% of your income a good idea? That depends on whether they are generating enough work and income for you. Taking on an agent or personal manager should not be a frivolous decision, and your awareness of their reputations, business style, contacts, and clients is crucial to your making the right choice. If you are thinking of hiring an agent or manager, consider the following guidelines:

- Agents not based in New York or L.A. may be at a disadvantage when it comes to submitting your work to the entertainment companies located in these major cities. Some agents who work regionally do have strong contacts and an established history in the business. Be sure to ask a regional agent or manager about the quality of his contacts in New York and Los Angeles.
- As a beginner, you have no clout in the business. Likewise, new agents who take on beginners don't have much influence. The only real service an inexperienced agent provides is an official-looking cover letter. While this doesn't sound like much, it's a great help, since many companies will not review work that isn't submitted by an agent.

- Getting an agent or manager is part of the difficult process of breaking into the business. Realize that the process of building your career will remain difficult, even after you get an agent or manager.
- Before signing an agreement with an agent or manager, review it with a lawyer. Long-term contracts are easy to sign and hard to break. You will have only one agent, but he will have many clients. If he doesn't work for you or return your calls, you're out of luck. If you do get a job, however, he will expect to collect. Going to court to plead your case is expensive. If you sign an agreement with an agent or manager, there should be a termination clause that allows either party to end the relationship with some immediacy. I recommend that you never allow anyone to sign off on a deal for you. Once you give someone power of attorney (the right to sign a contract on your behalf), you have basically relinquished having a say in what happens in your career. Whenever possible, do not allow others to collect money for you. Most publishers and entertainment companies will pay you and your agent separately.
- Review with a prospective agent or manager how he works with clients. After reading your work, can he present you with a long-term plan for your career? Does this plan make sense? Again, keep your ego in check and get answers to these questions. If an agent or manager begins by quoting

large sums of money, proceed cautiously. Find out why the agent or manager thinks your work is special and where he thinks he can sell it.

- Don't lend an agent money or listen to his personal problems. This is a business relationship. It is also unfair for you to expect your agent or manager to become your shrink and caretaker.

Some agents will work with you on an as-needed basis. They won't sign you up, but will negotiate deals for you. Agents negotiate as part of their daily business, and will probably be better at making sure you get a fair price. This may result in the agent having the opportunity to reassess your work and deciding to continue the relationship in a more formal way.

Education and Training Alternatives:

Schools, Classes, Internships, Volunteer Work, Summer Programs, Conferences, Seminars, Workshops and Continuing Education

There are a variety of institutions and organizations that can help you learn the craft of writing. While your dream may be to study with the "greats," many different kinds of classes, conferences, workshops, and seminars can teach you the basics of writing.

COLLEGES

If your focus is on writing, how do you select the college that's best for you? Ivy League schools with their glamorous traditions and networking possibilities are attractive choices, particularly if you have unlimited capital. Otherwise, you have to consider that writing, like acting, brings with it no assurances of paid employment.

If you have limited funds, you should consider applying to accredited colleges that can offer you the kind of liberal arts background you need to work in the various writing markets. Needless to say, there are an endless number of schools to choose from. As you make your selection, evaluate the following issues:

- Level of training offered. Look for a solid curriculum that offers exposure to different styles of writing and the business aspects of the field.
- Teaching staff. The professors should be people who have been active in the field of writing.
- Networking possibilities. Are the teachers and past students currently involved in the various writing markets? It is important to learn from people who have direct experience. Also, graduates who are active in the alumni organizations may be useful contacts.
- Internships. Schools that offer opportunities to work in television, film, publishing, and theater will give you an opportunity to get direct exposure and practical experience.
- Publishing opportunities. Does the school offer opportunities to write, publish, or present your work in school magazines, literary journals, and newspapers? Will you have a chance to see your plays and screenwriting presented on stage or video?

INTERNSHIPS AND VOLUNTEER WORK

Internships
Most schools offer internships at television stations, film companies, theaters, publishing houses, magazines, and newspapers. An internship offers you business experience and the chance to network with professionals. Use this

opportunity to build relationships. Some schools offer a wide variety of internships that count toward your course credits.

Unfortunately, interns get few job perks. You will probably be asked to deliver mail or coffee, do basic fact checking, type letters, and write copy. In short, the work may be on the menial side. Keep in mind you are there to see how the business works, not to be lauded for your writing genius. Although some internships may offer the student a small stipend or "lunch money," it's a rarity. An internship is a give-and-take situation. In exchange for your labor, you get invaluable exposure.

Volunteering

If you are unable to find an internship, offer your services as a volunteer to a company you'd like to work for. Many television and radio stations, theaters, publishing companies, nonprofit agencies, and arts groups have volunteer coordinators who can be contacted through their administrative offices. As with internships, a volunteer job can give you great exposure and a chance to beef up your resume.

THE WRITER'S VACATION

For the last 17 years I have been living a double life. In addition to my writing, I supervise an Intensive Psychiatric Rehabilitation Training program. I love my job, but

I also love writing. I use a great deal of my vacation time to pursue my writing.

Consider taking a few weeks off to take an intensive writing class. Many school programs feature summer classes in their undergraduate, graduate, and continuing education programs. These are great opportunities for immersing yourself in learning your craft. Peruse school catalogs for summer program listings and look for advertisements for writer's workshops in trade magazines.

SUMMER PROGRAM RESOURCES

The Yale Summer Writing Program, Yale University Yale Summer Programs, 246 Church St., Suite 101, New Haven CT 06510-1722. Tel: 203-432-2430. Offers five-week courses in fiction and nonfiction writing, screenwriting, and playwriting.

College of DuPage, 22nd St. and Lambert Road, Glen Ellyn IL 60137-6599. Tel: 708-942-2505. Offers eight-week courses in screenwriting and fiction writing.

Iowa Summer Writing Festival, The University of Iowa, Division of Continuing Education, 116 International Center, Iowa City IA 52242-1802. Tel: 314-335-2534. The summer schedule features one-week, four-day, and weekend workshops in fiction and nonfiction writing, and screenwriting.

CONFERENCES

A conference should offer what it promises—the opportunity to have a dialogue with professionals in the writing business. Obviously, this dialogue is not going to happen on a one-to-one basis. There should, however, be some satisfactory way of having your questions answered. This may involve a question-and-answer period or informal chances to mingle during lunch, dinner, or cocktails. Don't assume this will happen. Before attending, call the conference sponsor directly and ask if the speaker will be available to answer your questions.

SEMINARS

Seminars usually have a tighter focus on a specific area that involves writing or a topic of interest to writers. These can be held by a writers' group, an established publisher, a producer, or an industry specialist. The subjects of seminars may range from fiction and nonfiction writing to money management for creative types. Look for a seminar that focuses on your immediate needs, whether it's developing a project, getting an agent, or learning to work with an editor or producer. The seminar should present ideas and information that you need to further your career. Once again, scrutinize the brochure before attending.

WORKSHOPS

The point of attending a workshop is to progress with your work, and if a change of location will aid in that process, great! You can attend workshops that are close to home or in exotic locations. In either case, make sure you get feedback on your work and helpful advice on improving your writing skills and developing new projects.

PREPARING YOURSELF FOR THE CONFERENCE, SEMINAR, OR WORKSHOP:

- Do your homework. To get the most from the lecturers, research their work before the event and compare it to your own.
- Set goals for yourself. Outline the information you need or want. Make it your business to talk to presenters whose ideas and/or opinions you respect. Interact with other attendees who are writers. These events are great opportunities for making contact with other writers.
- Bring paper, pens, business cards, and your laptop. Take notes. You may be inundated with material or information, so don't risk forgetting it.
- Be comfortable. You might find yourself sitting in a cold, damp room all day. Bring a jacket or sweater, wear shoes that feel like slippers, bring a tote bag or briefcase for stowing papers.

RESOURCES

Hundreds of seminars, workshops, and conferences are offered every year and, if you read the trades in your targeted markets, you should have no trouble finding them. Evaluating them using the aforementioned criteria will ensure that each event you attend will help you grow as a writer. Some of the better known events include:

Readers' Digest Workshop, P. O. Box 5638, Flagstaff AZ 86011-5638. Tel: 602-523-3559. This workshop for freelance nonfiction writers is offered in several sites around the country. It provides information on working with specific publications.

The American Society of Journalists and Authors Spring Writer's Conference. 1501 Broadway, Suite 302, New York NY l0036. Tel: 212-997-0947. Having attended this annual event for several years, I learned invaluable information on writing for the nonfiction markets. This is geared for both beginning and seasoned writers.

The Writer's Network. 289 S. Robertson Blvd., Suite 465, Beverly Hills CA 90211. Tel: 800-64-NETWORK or 310-275-0287. This conference holds sessions on both coasts and offers presentations by leading writers, producers and agents in the television business.

Robert McKee's Story Structure. Two Arts, Inc., 12021 Wilshire Blvd., Suite 868, Los Angeles CA 90025. Tel:

310-312-1002. In New York, call: 212-463-7889. This film and television workshop is attended by professionals in all areas of the industry, as well as by beginning writers. It is presented in numerous locations around the country and in Europe. Call for schedules.

Michael Hauge's Screenwriting for Hollywood from Concept to Sale. P. O. Box 55728, Sherman Oaks CA 91413. Call 800-477-1947 for a schedule of upcoming events. Call 818-995-4209 for other inquiries. This broad-based conference on screenwriting is offered in many parts of the country several times a year.

Books

The Guide to Writers' Conferences edited by Dorlene Kaplan. $16.95. Shaw Guides, Inc., 10 W. 66th St., Suite 30H, New York NY 10021. To order, call 800-247-6553.

Networking at Writers' Conferences: From Contacts to Contracts by Steven D. Spratt and Lee G. Spratt. $12.95. John Wiley & Sons, Inc., Professional Reference and Trade Co., 605 3rd Avenue, New York NY 10158-0017.

Grants, Contests, and Fellowships

The writing life, especially when you are just starting out, brings with it financial concerns. To help with this, writers should research grants, contests, and fellowships that will assist them in supporting themselves while they're writing. If you read the trades, and network with other industry professionals, you will probably need no help in discovering where these opportunities exist. In general, you can find out about grants, contests, and fellowships through contacting writing organizations.

One clearing house for information is The Foundation Center, 79 5th Ave., New York NY 10003-3076, Tel: 212-620-4230. Through its publications, reference sources, and on-line services, this nonprofit organization provides information on writing jobs, fellowships and grants for writers, artists, and nonprofit agencies. This information is also available throughout the country via 200 cooperating libraries around the country, which work in conjunction with The Foundation Center. The Foundation Center provides referrals and also sponsors workshops and seminars that teach grant proposal writing.

RESOURCES

Grants and Awards Available to American Writers. $10.00. Pen America Center, 568 Broadway, New York NY 10012-3225. Tel: 212-334-1660.

Gadney's Guide to 1,800 International Contests, Festivals and Grants in Film, Video, Photography, Television, Radio Broadcasting, Writing, Poetry, Playwriting, and Journalism. $22.95. Festival Publications, 7944 Capistrano Avenue, West Hills CA 91304.

The Annual Register of Grant Support, A Directory of Funding Sources. $185.00. R.R. Bowker, Reed Reference Publishing, 121 Chanlon Road, New Providence NJ 07974. Check your local library for a copy.

Legal Issues

The most important message of this book is that you should take responsibility for your career. Discuss your work and your expectations with publishers, editors, producers, and directors prior to selling them the rights to your material. Find out if they expect you to make changes, if they plan to alter the material significantly, or hire someone else to do so, and how they plan to present it. This will allow you to make an informed decision as to whether you feel their alterations will enhance the work. This will also keep you from getting involved in a legal entanglement should your work be presented in a manner you find disagreeable. Once you sell the rights, it is difficult, if not impossible, to get them back.

The same is true for the business side of writing. It should never be assumed that signed contracts and copyright registration can be changed later. Protect your work before it is sold or, in the latter case, submitted. Having an agent or personal manager will not necessarily protect you. Many agents and managers don't understand the law or are dishonest. This is a business in which everyone is trying to make money for themselves. Never forget that.

LEGAL ADVICE: WHERE TO GET IT, EVEN IF YOU HAVE NO MONEY

If sale of your project earns you a healthy paycheck, or if you have an income from other sources, you should have no problem securing an attorney who specializes in your area of writing. This lawyer should be someone who is recommended to you by family, friends, or your network of writers and/or industry contacts. If you have been following the industry trades, you should have a sense of whom to contact. It may be unwise to accept referrals from your agent, publisher, or producer. The lawyers they recommend may be their acquaintances, and this could present a conflict of interest for you.

For most writers, hiring a private attorney isn't feasible. This does not mean that you should sign contracts without legal advice. There is an alternatives for artists and writers. Volunteer Lawyers for the Arts, VLA, has been providing legal assistance to artists and writers since 1969. The VLA Art Law Line (Tel: 212-319-2910 available 9:30 A.M.–4:30 P.M., Eastern Standard Time, Monday–Friday) will provide answers to arts-related questions, counseling, and a listing of volunteer attorneys. In addition, it offers information on small claims court proceedings, taxes, and constitutional issues. The VLA acts as a clearing house for other volunteer lawyer organizations and can refer you to one of 40 agencies nationwide who provide similar services.

As with contracts or legal agreements, your work

should be copyrighted prior to submission to protect you and save you from costly litigation later on.

To copyright your material, I suggest using The Writers Guild of America. Their service is fast and efficient. Send your material by registered mail.

RESOURCES

The Law (In Plain English) for Writers by Leonard D. Duboff, Professor of Law at Northwestern School of Law. $14.95. John Wiley & Sons, Inc., Professional Reference, Inc., Trade Group, 605 3rd Avenue, New York NY 10158-0017. Covers all laws governing book and magazine contracts, agents, copyrights, libel, invasion of privacy, taxes, self-publishing, and start-up businesses.

How to Register a Copyright and Protect Your Creative Work by Robert B. Chickering and Susan Hartman. $13.00. Charles Scribner's Sons, Macmillan Publishing Co., 866 3rd Avenue, New York NY 10022.

The Nature of Copyright: A Law of User's Rights by L. Ray Patterson and Stanley W. Lindburg. $12.95. University of Georgia Press, Athens GA 30602.

The Writers Guild of America. East Tel: 212-767-7800; West Tel: 310-550-1000. This organization offers registration services to protect your work. For members, it supplies industry practice and payment standards for contracts and negotiations, writing fellowships, symposiums, panel discussions, and awards programs. Call for details and membership criteria. The Writers Guild East covers writers who live east of the Mississippi. Writers living west of the Mississippi are covered by the Writers Guild West.

Writers' Groups

Discipline haunts every writer. Without it, even watching a *Gilligan's Island* rerun for the hundredth time seems like a better idea than staring down at a blank page. Novice writers are often plagued by anxiety and confidence problems. Often, the best antidote is a deadline, and this is why writers' groups can be beneficial. Meeting with other writers on a weekly basis will provide the structure that will help you build discipline. In addition, your writers' group will give you feedback on your writing. A group should be made up of no more than 10 members meeting once or twice a month. If the group is too large, individual attention is compromised.

The writers' group should not, however, engage in blistering attacks and mean-spirited criticism. Discussions of a writer's work should be about options. In short, successful writers' groups nurture and encourage the beginning writer.

If you want to join a writers' group, check local papers, writers' magazines, or school newsletters and bulletin boards for listings. If there is no group in your area, you may consider starting one. Whether you start a group or join an existing one, create guidelines that ensure that there's enough time for each writer to have individual attention and regulate the way criticism is conveyed. If a member seems overwhelmed by feedback, the discussion should be ended.

A final word of caution. Writers' groups, like studying with the same teacher, can reach a point of diminishing returns. Staying with one group for too long may inhibit the development of your own voice. Also, as you begin to work professionally, your concerns as a writer might not match the concerns of your group. Exposure is always the key. It may be time to move on or begin a new writers' group to stretch yourself and ensure the development of your own, unique voice.